NEW WAYS WITH DRIED FLOWERS

New Ways With Dried Flowers

50 Innovative

Dried Floral Designs

TEXT BY

FIONA BARNETT

AND

ROGER EGERICKX

PHOTOGRAPHY BY

DEBBIE PATTERSON

SMITHMARK

THIS EDITION PUBLISHED IN 1996 BY
SMITHMARK PUBLISHERS, A DIVISION OF U.S. MEDIA HOLDINGS INC.,
16 EAST 32ND STREET, NEW YORK, NY 10016.

SMITHMARK BOOKS ARE AVAILABLE FOR BULK PURCHASE FOR SALES
PROMOTION AND FOR PREMIUM USE.
FOR DETAILS WRITE OR CALL THE MANAGER OF SPECIAL SALES, SMITHMARK
PUBLISHERS, 16 EAST 32ND STREET, NEW YORK, NY 10016: (212) 532-6600

PREVIOUSLY PUBLISHED AS PART OF A LARGER COMPENDIUM,
THE NEW FLOWER ARRANGER

PRINTED AND BOUND IN SINGAPORE BY STAR STANDARD INDUSTRIES, PTE. LTD.

CONTENTS
· · ·

...

NEW WAYS WITH DRIED FLOWERS

...

Capture the very essence of Nature with these imaginative dried flower arrangements. From sweet-smelling posies of roses and lavender to spectacular floral wreaths and garlands, the following pages will show you how to create beautiful displays that will last for many months. Introducing a wide range of dried flowers, grasses and foliage as well as sea shells and starfish, the displays are lively and contemporary in feel and will challenge both beginner and expert alike.

INTRODUCTION
· · ·

Right: Dried Flower Tussie Mussies (page 82)

Above: Decorated Pot Display (page 26)

Right: Crescent Moon Wreath (page 92)

Dried flowers used to be thought of chiefly as a winter substitute for unavailable fresh blooms. But improvements in the technology of preserving plant materials has resulted in an increase in types of dried flowers and the introduction of vibrant new colours. The astonishing range of materials and colours now available has heralded a new dawn of possibilities in dried flower arranging.

Today's approach to dried flower displays is to emphasize colour and texture by using massed materials so that the collective strength of their qualities creates the impact. Even where a number of varieties are incorporated in a display they should be used in clusters to extract the maximum effect. It is wise to avoid using individual stems of a particular material because this will make for rather bitty looking displays.

To get the best out of dried plant material, do not be afraid to integrate other materials with them: dried fruits, gourds, seashells, roots and driftwood can all add an extra dimension to a display. To create an opulent effect, bunches of dried herbs and spices and varieties of dried and preserved mosses can be added and groups of filled terracotta pots may be attached. With all this choice today's dried

Above: Apple and Lavender Topiary Tree (page 28)

Left: Peony and Apple Table Arrangement (page 34)

flower display is a far cry from the fading brown and orange dust traps of the past.

Impressive though improvements in preserving plant materials may be, the ravages of time, sunlight, moisture and dust still take their toll on dried flowers. Do not make the mistake of believing dried arrangements will last for ever. A useful life of around six months is the best that can be expected before dried flowers begin to look dusty and faded.

However, by taking a few simple common sense precautions, the life of a dried arrangement can be maximized. To avoid fading, keep the arrangement out of direct sunlight. Do not allow dried flowers to become damp and particularly be aware of condensation in bathrooms and on window ledges. To prevent the build-up of dust give the arrangement an occasional blast with a hair-dryer set on slow and cool. When the arrangement is new, spray it with hair lacquer to help prevent the dropping of grass seeds and petals, but do not use hair-spray on dust-covered dried flowers.

Below: Rose and Starfish Wreath (page 36)

A potentially rewarding aspect of dried flower arranging is drying and preserving the plant material yourself. It takes patience and organization but with application you will be able to preserve materials not commercially available and, since some dried flowers can be expensive, you will save yourself money.

There are different methods of preservation to suit different plant materials. In the following pages, these methods are clearly explained. There is also a list of materials with the appropriate drying method for each. The list is not exhaustive so if the material you want to preserve is not referred to, then assess its characteristics, find a similar type and try the method recommended for that.

*Right: This contemporary
massed display would make a
powerful centrepiece for a
circular table.*

Below: A large Banksia
cookinea *forms the focal point
of this dried arrangement.*

*Below: The contrasting hues of
dried hydrangea heads blend
together beautifully in this
attractive circlet.*

BALANCE

Balance is very important in a flower display, both physically and visually. Foremost, the flower arranger must ensure the physical stability of the display. This involves understanding the mechanics of the arrangement, the types and sizes of materials used, how they are positioned and in what type of container. Different types of floral displays require different strategies to ensure their stability.

A large arrangement to be mounted on a pedestal will need a heavy, stable container. The display materials should be distributed evenly around the container and the weight concentrated as near the bottom as possible. Make sure the longer flowers and foliage do not cause the display to become top-heavy.

A mantelpiece arrangement can be particularly difficult to stabilise since the display materials hanging down over the shelf will tend to pull it forward. So use a heavy container and position the flowers and foliage as far back in it as possible.

Check the stability of an arrangement at regular stages during its construction.

Achieving a visual balance in a flower arrangement involves scale, proportion and colour as well as creating a focal point in the display.

The focal point of an arrangement is an area to which the eye should be naturally drawn and from which all display materials should appear to flow. While the position of the focal point will vary according to the type of display, generally speaking it will be towards its centre. This is where the boldest colours and shapes should be concentrated, with paler colours around the outside.

Always think of the display in three dimensions, never forgetting that as well as a front, it will have sides and a back. This is not difficult to remember for a bouquet or a free-standing, pedestal-mounted display, but can be forgotten if a display is set against a wall. Even a flat-backed arrangement needs depth and shape. Recessing materials around the focal point will help give it depth and weight.

Balance in a floral display is the integration of all visual factors to create a harmonious appearance and with practice you will develop the ability to achieve this.

SCALE AND PROPORTION

Scale is a very important consideration when planning a floral display.

In order to create an arrangement which is pleasing to the eye, the sizes of different flower types used in the same display should not be radically different. For example, it would be difficult to make amaryllis look in scale with lily-of-the-valley.

The type of foliage used should be in scale with the flowers, the display itself must be in scale with its container, and the arrangement and its container must be in scale with its surroundings. A display in a large space in a public building must itself be appropriately large enough to make a statement, conversely a bedside table would require no more than an arrangement in a bud vase.

Proportion is the relationship of width, height and depth within a floral display and in this respect there are some rule-of-thumb guidelines worth bearing in mind.
❖ In a tied bouquet, the length of the stems below the binding point should be approximately one-third of the bouquet's overall height.

❖ In a trailing wedding bouquet, the focal point of the display will probably be about one-third of the overall length up from its lowest point.

❖ For a pedestal arrangement, the focal point will be approximately two-thirds of the overall height down from its top-most point.

❖ A vase with long-stemmed flowers such as lilies, should be around one-third the height of the flowers.

❖ The focal point of a corsage is about one-third the overall height up from the bottom.

However, remember that decisions on the scale and proportion of a floral display are a matter of personal taste and thus will vary from person to person.

The important thing is not simply to accept a series of rules on scale and proportion but to give these factors your consideration and develop your own critical faculties in this area.

Above: Contrast is provided here by the apricot colour and geometric shape of the small dried starfish.

Top left: A strong geometric pattern has been achieved by the use of stacked rings of flowers of one type and colour.

COLOUR

The way in which colour is used can be vital to the success or failure of a display and there are several factors to bear in mind when deciding on a colour palette.

Though most people have an eye for colour, an understanding of the theory of colour is useful. Red, blue and yellow are the basic hues from which all other colours stem. Red, orange and yellow are warm colours which tend to create an exciting visual effect, while green, blue and violet are cooler and visually calmer.

Generally speaking, the lighter, brighter and hotter a colour, the more it will dominate an arrangement. White (which technically is the absence of colour) is also prominent in a display of flowers.

On the other hand, the darker and cooler the colour, the more it will visually recede into a display. It is important to bear this in mind when creating large displays to be viewed from a distance. In such circumstances blue and violet, in particular, can become lost in an arrangement.

Usually a satisfactory visual balance should be achieved if the stronger, bolder coloured flowers are positioned towards the centre of the display with the paler, more subtle colours around the outside.

Now armed with some basic knowledge of colour theory you can be braver in your choice of palette. "Safe" colour combinations such as creams with whites, or pinks with mauves have their place, but experiment with oranges and violets, yellows and blues, even pinks and yellows and you will add a vibrant dimension to your flower arranging.

Above: The exotic colours of the flowers in this wall sheath are perfectly offset by the beautiful ruby and gold ribbon.

Left: This bouquet reveals the strong natural colours now available in dried flowers.

CONTAINERS

. . .

While an enormous range of suitable, practical, purpose-made containers is available to the flower arranger, with a little imagination alternatives will present themselves, often in the form of objects we might not have at first glance expected. An old jug or teapot, a pretty mug that has lost its handle, an unusual-looking tin, a bucket, a jam jar, all these offer the arranger interesting opportunities.

Remember, if the container is for fresh flowers, it must be watertight or properly lined. Consider the scale and proportion of the container both to the particular flowers you are going to use, and the type of arrangement.

Do not forget the container can be a hidden part of the design, simply there to hold the arrangement, or it can be an integral and important feature in the overall arrangement.

BAKING TINS (PANS)
Apart from the usual round, square or rectangular baking tins (pans), a number of novelty shapes are available. Star, heart, club, spade and diamond shaped baking tins (pans) are used to make cakes that are out of the ordinary and they can also be used very effectively to produce interesting flower arrangements.

These tins (pans) are particularly good for massed designs, either of fresh or dried flowers, but remember, the tin may need lining if it is being used for fresh flowers.

BASKETS
Baskets made from natural materials are an obvious choice for country-style, informal displays. However, there is a wide range of basket designs available to suit many different styles.

Large baskets are good for table or static displays while smaller baskets

Massed flowerheads in this baking tin (pan) produce a striking display.

with handles can be carried by bridesmaids or filled with flowers or plants and made into lovely gifts. Traditional wicker baskets can be obtained which incorporate herbs or lavender in their weave.

Wire or metal baskets offer an ornate alternative to wicker and twig, since the wire can be formed into intricate shapes and also can have a more modern look.

CAST-IRON URNS
More expensive than many other types of container, the investment in a cast-iron urn is repaid by the splendid classic setting it offers for the display of flowers. Whether the arrangement is large and flowing or contemporary and linear, the visual strength of a classical urn shape will provide the necessary underpinning.

Of course the physical weight of a cast-iron urn is a factor to consider; it is a plus in that it will remain stable with the largest of displays but a minus when it comes to moving it!

ENAMELLED CONTAINERS
The appeal of using an enamelled container probably lies in the bright colours available. Containers in strong primary colours work well with similarly brightly coloured flowers to produce vibrant displays.

GALVANIZED METAL BUCKET AND POT
The obvious practical advantage of galvanized metal containers is that they will not rust. The attractive silvered and polished texture is ideal for contemporary displays in both fresh and dried flowers.

Today lots of shapes and sizes of containers are available with a galvanized finish but even an old-fashioned bucket can be used to good effect in flower arranging.

GLASS VASES
A glass vase is often the first thing that springs to mind for flower arranging. And indeed, there is an enormous range of purpose-made vases available.

The proportions of this design give prominence to the classical urn.

A varied selection from the vast range of containers that can be used for flower arranging.

Particularly interesting to the serious flower arranger will be simple clear glass vases which are made in all the sizes and geometric shapes you could ever need. Their value lies in their lack of embellishment which allows the arrangement to speak for itself. Remember the clear glass requires that the water be changed regularly and kept scrupulously clean, since below the water is also part of the display.

There are also many other forms of vase – frosted, coloured, textured, and cut glass – and all have their place in the flower arranger's armoury.

PITCHERS

Pitchers of all types are ideal flower receptacles. Ceramic, glass, enamelled or galvanized metal; short, tall, thin, fat – whatever their shape, size or colour, they offer the flower arranger a wide range of options.

Displays can range from the rustic and informal to the grand and extravagant, depending on your choice of pitcher and materials.

PRE-FORMED PLASTIC FOAM SHAPES

Clean to handle, convenient to use, pre-formed plastic foam comes in a wide range of shapes and sizes such as circles, crosses, rectangles and even "novelty" designs like stars, numerals, hearts and teddy bears. Each shape is a moisture-retaining foam with a watertight backing. Equivalent foam shapes are available for dried flowers.

Although often associated with funeral and sympathy designs, pre-formed plastic foam shapes also offer the flower arranger a variety of bases for many other types of display.

TERRACOTTA PLANT POTS

Traditional or modern, the terracotta pot can be utilized to hold an arrangement of flowers and not just plants. If the arrangement is built in plastic foam, line the pot with cellophane (plastic wrap) before

inserting the foam, to prevent leakage. Alternatively just pop a jam jar or bowl into the pot to hold the water.

The appearance of terracotta pots can be changed very effectively by techniques such as rubbing them with different coloured chalks, or treating them with gold leaf. They can also be aged by the application of organic materials such as sour milk which, if left, will enable a surface growth to develop.

WOODEN TRUGS AND BOXES

Old-fashioned wooden trugs and seedboxes can make charming and effective containers for floral displays. Their rustic appeal makes them particularly suitable for informal country-style designs where the container is an enhancing feature. Rubbing the surface of a wooden container with coloured chalk can create an entirely new look.

Of course you must remember to line the box with waterproof material if fresh flowers or plants are going to be used in the display.

EQUIPMENT

• • •

The flower arranger can get by with the minimum of equipment when he or she is just starting out. However, as he or she becomes more adventurous, a selection of specialized tools and equipment will be useful. This section itemizes those pieces of equipment used in the projects contained in the book.

CELLOPHANE (PLASTIC WRAP)

As wrapping for a bouquet, cellophane (plastic wrap) can transform a bunch of flowers into a lovely gift, and it has a more practical use as a waterproof lining for containers. Also, it can look very effective scrunched up in a vase of water to support flower stems.

FLORIST'S ADHESIVE

This very sticky glue is supplied in a pot and is the forerunner to the hot, melted adhesive of the glue gun. It is necessary when attaching synthetic ribbons or other materials which might be adversely affected by the heat of a glue gun.

FLORIST'S ADHESIVE TAPE

This is a strong adhesive tape used to secure plastic foam in containers. Although it will stick under most circumstances, avoid getting it too wet as this will limit its adhesive capability.

PLASTIC FOAM

Plastic foam comes in a vast range of shapes, sizes and densities, and is available for both dry and fresh flowers. While the rectangular brick is the most familiar, other shapes are available for specific purposes.

Plastic foam is lightweight, convenient to handle and very easy to cut and shape with just a knife. A brick of plastic foam for fresh flowers soaks up water very quickly

Before starting to build a design make sure you have all the materials close to hand.

(approximately 1½ minutes) but must not be resoaked as the structure alters and its effectiveness will be reduced. Plastic foam for dried flowers can seem too hard for the delicate stems of some flowers but a softer version is available, so consider which type you need before starting the design.

FLORIST'S SCISSORS

A strong, sharp pair of scissors are the flower arranger's most important tool. As well as cutting all those things you would expect, the scissors must also be sturdy enough to cut woody stems and even wires.

FLORIST'S TAPE (STEM-WRAP TAPE)

This tape is not adhesive, but the heat of your hands will help secure it to itself as it is wrapped around a stem

The tape is used to conceal wires and seal stem ends. It is made either from plastic or crêpe paper and it will stretch to provide a thin covering. The tape is available in a range of colours although green is normally used on fresh flowers.

FLORIST'S WIRE

Wire is used to support, control and secure materials, also to extend stems and to replace them where weight reduction is required. The wire tends to be sold in different lengths. Most of the projects in this book use 36 cm (14 in) lengths. Always use the lightest gauge of wire you can while still providing sufficient support. The most popular gauges are:

1.25mm (18g)	0.28mm (31g)
0.90mm (20g)	0.24mm (32g)
0.71mm (22g)	Silver reel
0.56mm (24g)	*(rose) wires:*
0.46mm (26g)	0.56mm (24g)
0.38mm (28g)	0.32mm (30g)
0.32mm (30g)	0.28mm (32g)

Make sure that the wires are kept in a dry place because any moisture will cause them to rust.

GLOVES

While some flower arranging processes would be impeded by gloves, it makes sense to protect your hands whenever necessary, especially if handling materials with sharp thorns or sap which might irritate the skin. So keep some domestic rubber gloves and heavy-duty gardening gloves in your florist's workbox.

GLUE GUN

The glue gun is an electrically powered device fed by sticks of glue, which it melts to enable the user to apply glue via a trigger action. In floristry it is a relatively recent development but invaluable in allowing the arranger to attach dried or fresh materials to swags, garlands or circlets securely, cleanly and efficiently.

The glue and the tip of the gun are extremely hot, so take care at all times when using a glue gun. Never leave a hot glue gun unattended.

PAPER RIBBON

Paper ribbon is an alternative to satin and synthetic ribbon and is available in a large range of mostly muted, soft

colours. It is sold twisted and rolled up. Cut the length of ribbon required in its twisted state and carefully untwist and flatten it to its full width before creating your bow.

PINHOLDER

The pinholder is a heavy metal disc approximately 2 cm (¾ in) thick which has an even covering of sharp metal pins, approximately 3 cm (1¼ in) long. Pinholders are available in a range of diameter sizes for different displays.

The pinholder is placed under the water and the bottom of the flower stems are pushed on to the pins. The weight of the stems is balanced by the weight of the pinholder. It is ideal for creating *Ikebana*-style displays or twiggy linear arrangements.

RAFFIA

A natural alternative to string and ribbon, raffia has several uses for the flower arranger. It can be used, a few strands at a time, to tie together a hand-arranged, spiralled bunch, or to attach bunches of dried or fresh

Start with the basic equipment and add items as your skill develops.

flowers to garlands and swags. In thicker swathes it can also be used to finish bouquets and arrangements by tying them off and being formed into decorative bows.

ROSE STRIPPER

This ingenious little device is a must when handling very thorny roses. Squeeze the metal claws together and pull the stripper along the stem, and the thorns and leaves will be removed. There is also a blade attachment to cut stem ends at an angle. Always wear thick gardening gloves.

SATIN RIBBON

Available in a large variety of widths and colours, satin ribbon is invaluable to the flower arranger when a celebratory final touch is required.

Satin ribbon is preferable to synthetic ribbon because it looks and feels so much softer. Its only drawback is that it frays when cut.

SECATEURS (GARDEN CLIPPERS)

These are necessary to cut the tougher, thicker stems and branches of foliage. Always handle scissors and secateurs with care and do not leave within the reach of young children.

TWINE

String or twine is essential when tying spiralled bunches, making garlands or attaching foliage to gates and posts.

WIRE MESH

Although plastic foam now offers much more flexibility for the flower arranger, wire mesh still has its place in the florist's armoury.

When creating large displays, wire mesh is essential to strengthen the plastic foam and prevent it from crumbling when large numbers of stems are pushed into it. The mesh should be cut in lengths from the roll, crumpled slightly, laid over the top and wrapped around the sides of the foam and wedged between it and the container, then secured in place with florist's adhesive tape.

WIRING TECHNIQUES

· · ·

TAPING

Stems and wires are covered with florist's tape (stem-wrap tape) for three reasons: first, cut materials which have been wired can no longer take up water and covering with tape seals in the moisture that already exists in the plant; second, the tape conceals the wires, which are essentially utilitarian, and gives a more natural appearance to the false stem; third, wired dried materials are covered with florist's tape (stem-wrap tape) to ensure that the material does not slip out of the wired mount.

1 Hold the wired stem near its top with the end of a length of florist's tape (stem-wrap tape) between the thumb and index finger of one hand. With your other hand, hold the remainder of the length of tape at 45° to the wired stem, keeping it taut. Starting at the top of the stem, just above the wires, rotate the flower slowly to wrap the tape around both the stem and wires, working down. By keeping it taut, the tape will stretch into a thin layer around the stem and wires. Each layer should overlap and stick to the one before. If you wish, you may add flowerheads at different heights as you tape to create units. Finally, fasten off just above the end of the wires by squeezing the tape against itself to stick it securely.

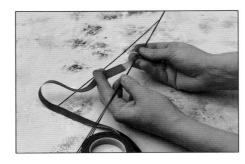

MAKING A STAY WIRE

1 Group together four .71 wires, each overlapping the next by about 3 cm (1¼ in). Start taping the wires together from one end using florist's tape (stem-wrap tape). As the tape reaches the end of the first wire add another .71 wire to the remaining three ends of wire and continue taping, and so on, adding wires and taping four together until you achieve the required length of stay wire.

SINGLE LEG MOUNT

This is for wiring flowers which have a strong natural stem or where a double weight of wire is not necessary to support the material.

1 Hold the flowers or foliage between the thumb and index finger of one hand while taking the weight of the material across the top of the same hand. Position a wire of the appropriate weight and length behind the stem about one-third up

from the bottom. Bend the wire ends together with one leg shorter than the other. Holding the short wire leg parallel with the stem, wrap the long wire leg firmly around both the stem and the other wire leg several times to secure. Straighten the long wire leg to extend the stem. Cover the stem and wire with florist's tape (stem-wrap tape).

DOUBLE LEG MOUNT

This is formed in the same way as the single leg mount but extends the stem with two equal length wire legs.

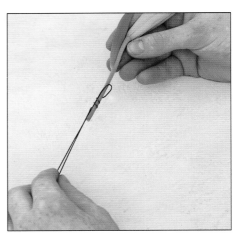

1 Hold the flower or foliage between the thumb and index finger of one hand while taking the weight of the plant material across the top of the same hand. Position a wire of appropriate weight and length behind the stem about one-third of the way up from the bottom. One-third of the wire should be to one side of the stem with two-thirds to the other. Bend the wire parallel to the stem. One leg will be about twice as long as the other.

Holding the shorter leg against the stem, carefully wrap the longer leg around both the stem and the other wire to secure. Finally, straighten both legs which should now be of equal length.

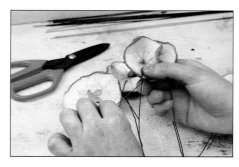

Preserved (dried) apple slices require careful handling when wiring.

WIRING A ROSE HEAD

Roses have relatively thick, woody stems so to make them suitable for use in intricate work, such as buttonholes, headdresses and corsages, the natural stem will need to be replaced with a wire stem.

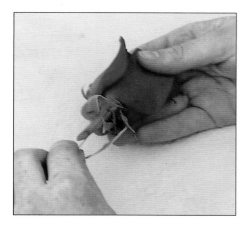

1 Cut the stem of the rose to a length of about 3 cm (1¼ in). Push one end of a .71 wire through the seed box of the rose at the side. Holding the head of the rose carefully in one hand (as it is very fragile), wrap the wire several times firmly around and down the stem. Straighten the remaining wire to extend the natural stem. Cover the wire and stem with florist's tape (stem-wrap tape).

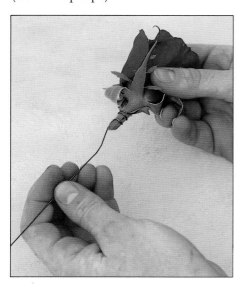

WIRING FRUIT AND VEGETABLES

Using fruit and vegetables in swags, wreaths and garlands, or securing them in plastic foam displays will require wiring them first. The method will depend on the item to be wired and how it is to be used.

Heavy fruits and vegetables, such as oranges, lemons or bulbs of garlic, will need a heavy .71 wire or even .90. The wire should be pushed through the item, just above its base from one side to the other. Push another wire through the item at right angles to the first and bend all four projecting wires to point downwards.

1 Depending on how the fruit or vegetables will be used, either cut the wires to a suitable length to be pushed into plastic foam, or twist the wires together to form a single stem.

2 Small delicate fruits and vegetables such as mushrooms or figs need careful handling as their flesh is easily damaged. They normally only need one wire. Push the wire through the

base of the item from one side to the other and bend the two projecting wires downwards. Depending on how the material is to be used, either twist to form a single stem, or trim to push into plastic foam.

For the soft materials .71 is the heaviest weight of wire you will require. In some instances, fruit or vegetables can be attached or secured in an arrangement by pushing a long wire "hairpin" right through the item and into the plastic foam behind.

3 Fruit or vegetables that have a stem, such as bunches of grapes or artichokes, can be double leg mounted on their stems with appropriate weight wires.

Extend the length of a starfish by double leg mounting one of its legs.

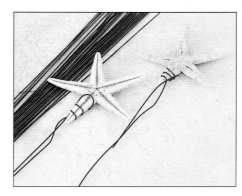

DRYING TECHNIQUES
· · ·

AIR DRYING

Probably the simplest method of preserving plant material is to air dry it. Air drying is the generic term for a number of techniques but fundamentally it is the preservation of plant materials without the use of chemicals or desiccants.

The ideal environment for air drying will be dark, warm, clean, dust-free, well ventilated and, most importantly, dry. Typically, attics, boiler rooms or large airing cupboards are the locations where these conditions are found.

HARVESTING MATERIALS

If you are preserving material you have grown yourself, be sure it is as dry as possible when you harvest it. Choose a dry day after the morning dew has disappeared and before the damp of evening begins to settle.

It is also important to harvest materials at the right point in their development, to ensure colours remain vibrant and petals do not drop. Experience will teach you about any variations from plant to plant, but in general the time to harvest is when the material is neither too young nor too mature – when the flowers have developed from bud to open bloom but are still young, fresh and firm. Seed pods and grasses must be just

Selecting the right drying method for a plant comes with experience.

fully developed - any more and the seeds may drop.

If you buy commercially grown materials to dry yourself, bear in mind the general principles of harvesting when you select them, and remember, drying must take place as soon as possible after harvesting or purchasing the plant materials.

AIR DRYING BY HANGING PLANT MATERIAL

In most instances the foliage on flowers does not dry as well as the blooms so, when your materials are fresh, remove the leaves from the lower half of the stems before drying.

As a rule plant materials are bunched together in groups of not more than 10 stems and each bunch should contain only one plant variety. Stems should be all around the same length with all their heads at the same level. Do not pack the heads too tightly together as this will inhibit the circulation of air around them and may distort their final dried shape.

Secure the stem ends together with twine, raffia or a rubber band. The stems will shrink as they dry so a rubber band is probably most practical because it will contract with them to maintain a firm hold.

Hang the bunches in a suitable environment in a safe position, high enough so that they will not be disturbed and with their heads down and stems vertical.

Drying rates vary from plant to plant and are subject to factors such as atmospheric conditions, bunch sizes and temperatures but it is essential that you make sure the materials are thoroughly dried before using them. This will be when the thickest part of the flowerhead has dried and when bending the stem causes it to snap. Any moisture retained in plant

The weight of the flowerheads help keep the stems straight.

materials will cause mould, resulting in drooping and shrivelling.

It should be noted that some materials which can be dried with this method should not be hung with their heads down. In particular physalis, with its pendulous orange Chinese lanterns, would look unnatural if dried upside-down. Instead, hook individual physalis stems over a horizontal length of twine in their upright growing attitude.

AIR DRYING PLANT MATERIAL ON A RACK

Some plants such as *Daucus cariba* (Queen Anne's lace) can be air dried, but their florets will curl up if they are hung upside-down.

Instead, make a rack from a piece of small mesh wire, place it in a suitable environment, and drop the stem down through the mesh so that it is held by its bloom. With the flower facing upwards, it will dry well.

Hydrangea heads and gypsophila can both be air dried with their stems in water.

AIR DRYING PLANT MATERIALS WITH THEIR STEM ENDS IN WATER

This is the method of preservation for those types of flowers which have a tendency to wilt before the drying process is completed. It is sometimes called the "evaporation technique" and is particularly suitable for hydrangea, allium and heather.

Cut the bottoms of stems at an angle of 45 degrees and place them in a container with a depth of about 7.5 cm (3 in) of water and place the container in a suitable environment. This slows down the drying process to give the plant material time to dry fully in a natural position and without deterioration in the condition of the blooms.

AIR DRYING IN A "NATURAL" ATTITUDE

Some materials benefit from being dried in an upright position so that they retain a more natural shape.

Simply stand the material in the sort of container in which you might make an arrangement, place it in a suitable environment and it will dry in its natural shape. Grasses and stems of mimosa are suitable for this method.

However, with some material this method can produce extraordinary results. The normally straight stems of bear grass *(Xerophyllum tenax)* will,

when placed in a short container, form themselves into attractive ringlets as they dry. A simple alternative method for drying grasses is to lie them flat on paper in a suitable environment and they will retain a satisfactory shape.

DESICCANT DRYING

A particularly effective method of preservation is drying by the use of a desiccant such as sand, borax or, best of all, silica gel. The desiccant absorbs all the moisture from the plant material. This can be a time-consuming process but it is well worth the effort because the result is dried materials, with colour and form nearer their fresh condition than can be achieved by almost any other method of preservation.

This method is essential for the preservation of fleshy flowerheads that cannot be successfully air dried. Flowers such as lilies, tulips, freesias, pansies and open garden roses all respond well to desiccant drying and provide the flower arranger with a wealth of preserved materials not generally commercially available.

For the flower arranger there is little point in using this method for flower materials that air dry well because on a non-commercial scale desiccant drying is only suitable for small amounts of material and silica gel is expensive.

Flowers to be preserved by this method must be in perfect, healthy condition and harvested preferably after a few hours in the sun, with as little surface moisture as possible.

It is important to choose a drying method which will allow the plant material to retain its original colour and form.

There are flowers and materials from every season suitable for drying.

WIRING FLOWERS FOR DESICCANT DRYING

Desiccant drying is normally only used for flowerheads as the process weakens stems to the extent that they become virtually unusable. Also, it should be remembered that the flowerheads themselves will become very fragile. Indeed, if you are going to make wire stems it should be done while the flowers are still fresh before beginning the desiccant process.

Flowers with hollow stems, like zinnias, are wired by inserting the wire through their natural stem and pushing it into the flowerhead. Be careful not to push it too far because the flowerhead will shrink as it dries and this might expose an unsightly wire. Heavy petalled flowers like dahlias have to be dried face up, so only provide them with short wired stems. These stems can be extended after the flowers have been dried. Flowers which have woody, tough or very thin stems may be wired through the seed box (calyx) at the base of the flowerhead from one side to the other. Bring the projecting wire ends down and form them into a mount.

During the drying process the flower and stem will shrink so a double or single leg mount will become loose and slide off unless its wire has been securely pushed into the stem while the flower was still fresh. Remember that you still need to make the gauge of wire used for a mount compatible with the weight of the flower when it is fresh.

DRYING WITH SILICA GEL

Nowadays silica gel is considered a superior material to borax or sand for desiccant drying. Sand and borax are heavy and great care must be taken to avoid damaging flowers dried in these materials. Silica gel on the other hand is lightweight and can be crushed very fine so it can be worked into complicated petal configurations without causing damage.

Flowers dry very quickly in silica gel, five to ten days being the usual time necessary for most plant material. Borax and sand are much slower and it can take up to five weeks to dry some materials! Use an airtight container when using silica gel as it absorbs moisture from the air, whereas sand and borax can be used in any container provided it has a lid. The method for sand and borax is generally the same as for silica gel.

Some silica gel crystals are blue and this changes to pink as they absorb moisture which will help you measure the progress of the drying process.

1 When you have prepared your silica gel crystals place a layer approximately 5 cm (2 in) deep in the bottom of your container. Place the flowerheads in the crystals face down or if the petals are complex face up. If their stems are wire mounted, bend them as necessary to fit the flowers into the container.

2 When all flowerheads are in position, spoon a second 5 cm (2 in) deep layer of silica gel over them to cover completely. Be sure to fill all parts of the flowerhead with crystals. If it has complex petals, lift them carefully with a toothpick and gently push the crystals into every crevice. Put the lid on the container and tape around to make airtight.

Since each flower type will probably require a different time to dry, check progress at regular intervals. Flowers left too long in a desiccant will eventually disintegrate. When you start using this method, there will, of course, be an element of trial and error before you are able to establish the time necessary for each flower type.

Some flowers with a deep cupped shape, such as tulips, should be dried individually in a plastic cup of crystals sealed with clear film to ensure they keep their shape.

After you remove the dried flowers from the silica gel, they will probably still have powder on them and this must be removed very carefully with a fine, soft paintbrush.

You can, of course, re-use the silica gel over and over again. All you need to do is spread it out on a tray and leave it in a warm oven until it is dry. This will be easy to recognize in the coloured silica because it will become blue again.

MICROWAVE METHOD

The silica gel process can be accelerated by using a microwave oven. Remember, however, that you must not put wired materials in a microwave oven. Any wiring will have to be done after drying which may be difficult given the fragility of the dried blooms.

Bury the material in silica gel in a container, but do not put a lid on it. Instead, place the uncovered container in the microwave oven with about half a cup of water next to it.

Set the microwave timer according to the type of flower you are drying. Delicate blooms may take less than two minutes while more fleshy flowers will take longer. You will need to experiment with your timing to get accurate settings. After the process is ended leave the silica to cool before removing the flowers.

STORAGE OF DESICCANT DRIED MATERIALS

To keep desiccant dried materials in good condition store them in an airtight container, packed loosely with layers of tissue paper inbetween.

Place a small pouch of silica gel in the container to absorb any moisture, taking care not to get the silica in direct contact with the flowers.

Of course, there are plenty of materials dried by Nature to try in a display.

PRESERVING WITH GLYCERINE

1 Foliage in particular does not respond well to air drying. Its green colours fade and the result is tired-looking, brittle material. Happily the use of glycerine works well for many varieties of foliage.

This method enables plant material to replace the moisture which has evaporated from its stems and leaves by absorption of a solution of glycerine and water.

Because this process relies on the ability of plant material to draw up the solution it is not suitable for autumn foliage which has, of course, already died. Indeed, it is important that materials to be treated with glycerine are harvested in the middle of their growing season, when the leaves are young but developed and are full of moisture. Foliage that is too young and is soft and pale green does not respond to glycerine.

The stem ends of material to be treated should be cut at an angle of 45 degrees and the lower leaves stripped. Peel the bark off the bottom 6 cm (2½ in) of the stem and split the end up to about 10 cm (4 in) to ensure efficient absorption of the solution.

Mix one part glycerine with two parts hot water and pour the solution into a substantial container to a depth of about 20 cm (8 in). The size of container will depend on the amount of material to be treated. Stand the stems of foliage in the solution for anything from two to six weeks, depending on the size and texture of the leaves, to achieve full absorption. Always keep an eye on the amount of solution in the container and top it up as necessary to maintain the level.

2 If you are treating individual leaves they can be completely submerged in the solution, but a thicker half-glycerine, half-water mixture should be used. It will take two to three weeks for leaves to be properly treated, after which time remove them from the solution and wipe off any excess.

Glycerine treatment works best for mature, sturdy plant material such as beech, hornbeam, magnolia and elaeagnus. Surprisingly it is also successful with less robust material like *Molucella laevis* (bells of Ireland) and trails of ivy.

As materials are preserved their leaves will change colour to a variety of shades of brown. When all the leaves have changed colour you will know the process is complete. The visual results on materials of treatment with glycerine may vary even for the same material but with increasing experience of the technique you will become better able to predict what you are likely to achieve. Berried foliage can also be preserved with glycerine but the berries will shrink slightly and change colour.

An advantage of glycerine-preserved foliage is that it remains malleable, and dusty leaves can be wiped with a damp cloth.

PLANT PRESERVATION TECHNIQUES
· · ·

The following is a list of plants and materials and the drying method suitable for each. The list is not exhaustive, so if you find a plant you wish to try drying, assess its characteristics, find a similar type and try the drying method for that.

COMMON NAME	LATIN NAME	PLANT SECTION	TECHNIQUE
African marigold	*Tagetes*	flower	air drying
anemone (windflower)	*Anemone*	flower	air drying desiccant
asparagus	*Asparagus plumosus*	leaf	microwave
aspidistra	*Aspidistra*	leaf	glycerine
astilbe	*Astilbe*	flower	air drying
bay	*Laurus*	leaf	desiccant/glycerine
bear's breeches	*Acanthus*	flower spike / leaf	air drying / glycerine
beech	*Fagus*	leaf	glycerine
bellflower	*Campanula*	flower	air drying
bell heather	*Erica cinerea*	flower	air drying
bells of Ireland	*Molucella laevis*	bract	air drying/glycerine
blackberry (bramble)	*Robus (Rosaceae)*	leaf / berry	glycerine
blanket flower	*Gaillardia*	seedhead	air drying
broom	*Cytisus*	flower spray	air drying/desiccant
bulrush	*Typha latifolia*	seedhead	air drying
buttercup	*Ranunculus*	flower	desiccant
camellia	*Camellia*	flower	desiccant
campion (catchfly)	*Silene*	flower	air drying
candytuft	*Iberis*	flower / seedhead	dessicant / air drying
caraway	*Carum carvi*	seedhead	air drying
carnation	*Dianthus*	flower	desiccant
celosia	*Celosia*	flower	air drying/ air drying in water
chamomile	*Chamaemelum nobile Athemis*	flower	air drying/ air drying in water
Chinese lantern	*Physalis*	stems and seedheads	air drying
chive	*Allium schoenoprasum*	flower	air drying/ air drying in water
choisya	*Choisya*	leaf	glycerine
chrysanthemum	*Chrysanthemum*	flower	desiccant
clarkia	*Clarkia (syn Godetia)*	flower	air drying
clematis (old man's beard, travellers' joy)	*Clematis*	leaf / seedhead	air drying / air drying

COMMON NAME	LATIN NAME	PLANT SECTION	TECHNIQUE
cock's-foot grass	*Dactylis glomerata*	stems and seedheads	air drying
copper beech	*Fagus sylvatica*	leaf	air drying/glycerine
cornflower (bluebottle)	*Centaurea cyanus*	flower	air drying/ microwave/ air drying in water
corn cob	*Zea mays*	seedhead	air drying
cotinus	*Cotinus*	flower / leaf	air drying / glycerine
cow parsley	*Anthriscus sylvestris*	seedhead	air drying
daffodil	*Narcissus*	flower	desiccant
dahlia	*Dahlia*	flower	desiccant
daisy	*Bellis*	flower	desiccant
delphinium	*Delphinium*	flower spike	air drying/desiccant
dock	*Rumex*	seedhead	air drying
dryandra	*Dryandra*	flower	air drying
elaeagnus	*Elaeagnus*	leaf	glycerine/ microwave
eucalyptus	*Eucalyptus*	leaf	air drying/glycerine
fennel	*Foeniculum vulgare*	leaf / seedhead	air drying microwave / air drying
ferns		leaf	glycerine
fescue grass	*Festuca*	stems and seedheads	air drying
feverfew	*Chrysanthemum parthenium*	flower	air drying/ air drying in water/ microwave
fig	*Ficus*	leaf	glycerine
forsythia	*Forsythia*	flower sprays	desiccant
foxglove	*Digitalis*	flower	desiccant
freesia	*Freesia*	flower	desiccant
gay feathers	*Liatris*	flower spikes	air drying
geranium (cranesbill)	*Geranium*	leaf and flower	desiccant
giant hogweed	*Heracleum mantegazzianum*	stem and seedhead	air drying
globe amaranth	*Gomphrena globosa*	flowers	air drying
globe thistle	*Echinops*	thistle heads	air drying
golden rod	*Solidago*	flower	air drying microwave
grape hyacinth	*Muscari*	flower	desiccant
gypsophila	*Gypsophila*	flower	air drying/ air drying in water/ microwave
hare's-tail grass	*Lagarus ovatus*	stems and seedheads	air drying
heather	*Erica*	flower spikes	air drying in water/ glycerine
helichrysum	*Helichrysum*	flower	air drying
holly	*Ilex*	leaf	glycerine
hollyhock	*Alcea*	flower	desiccant
honesty	*Lunaria*	seedhead	air drying
hop	*Humulus*	leaf and bracts	air drying/glycerine
hosta (plantain lily)	*Hosta*	leaf	glycerine

COMMON NAME	LATIN NAME	PLANT SECTION	TECHNIQUE
hyacinth	Hyacinthus	flower	desiccant
hydrangea	Hydrangea	flower and bracts	air drying/ air drying in water/ microwave
ivy	Hedera	leaf	glycerine
Japanese aralia	Fatsia japonica	leaf	glycerine
Jerusalam sage	Phlomis fruticosa	flower, leaf and seedhead	air drying
kerria (Jew's mallow)	Kerria	flowers	air drying
knapweed	Centaurea	seedhead	air drying
lady's mantle	Alchemilla mollis	flower	air drying/ microwave
larkspur	Consolida	flower spike	air drying/desiccant
laurel	Laurus	leaf	glycerine
lavender	Lavandula	flower spikes	air drying/ air drying in water
lavender cotton	Santolina chamaecyparissus	leaf	air drying/ microwave
lilac	Syringa	small flower sprays	desiccant
lily	Lilium	flower	desiccant
lily-of-the-valley	Convallaria	flower	desiccant
linseed	Linum usitatissium	stems and seedheads	air drying
London pride	Saxifraga x urbium	flower	desiccant
Love-in-a-mist	Nigella damascena	flower and seedhead	air drying
love-lies-bleeding	Amaranthus caudatus	flower spike	air drying
lupin	Lupinus	flower	desiccant
		seedhead	air drying
magnolia	Magnolia	flower	desiccant
maple	Acer	leaf	glycereine
marguerite	Chrysanthemum frutescens	flower	desiccant
marjoram	Origanum	flower	air drying microwave
Mexican giant hyssop	Agastache	flower	air drying
millet	Panicum miliaceum	seedhead	air drying
mimosa	Acacia	flower sprays	air drying/desiccant air drying in water
mullein	Verbascum	seedhead	air drying
narcissus	Narcissus	flower	glycerine
oats	Avena sativa	stems and seedheads	air drying
onion	Allium	flower	air drying in water/ air drying
orchid	Orchidacea	flower	desiccant
pampas grass	Cortaderia selloana	stems and seedheads	air drying
pansy	Viola wittrockiana	flower	desiccant
pearl everlasting	Anaphalis	flower	air drying/ air drying in water
peony	Paeonia	flower	air drying/desiccant
pine	Pinus	cones	air drying
pinks	Dianthus	flower	desiccant
polyanthus	Primula	flower	desiccant
poppy	Papaver	seedhead	air drying
pot marigold	Calendula officinalis	flower	air drying/desiccant
phalaris	Phalaris	stems and seedheads	air drying

COMMON NAME	LATIN NAME	PLANT SECTION	TECHNIQUE
primrose	Primula vulgaris	flower	desiccant
quaking grass	Briza	stems and seedheads	air drying upright or hanging
rhododendron	Rhododendron	leaf	glycerine microwave
rose	Rosa	bud, flower, leaf	air drying
		fully open flower	dessicant
		hip	glycerine
rosemary	Rosmarinus officinalis	leaf spike	glycerine/air drying microwave
rue	Ruta graveolens	seedhead	air drying
safflower	Carthamus tinctorius	flower	air drying
sage	Salvia officinalis	flower and leaf	air drying
sea holly	Eryngium	flower	air drying
sea lavender	Limonium	flower	air drying/ air drying in water
sedge	Carex	seedhead	air drying
sedum (stonecrop)	Sedum	flower	air drying/desiccant microwave
senecio	Senecio	leaf	air drying/ microwave
shoofly	Nicandra phyusalodes	seedpods	air drying
sorrel tree	Oxydendrum arboreum	seedhead	air drying
statice	Psylliostachys	flower	air drying
stock	Matthiola	flower	dessicant
strawflower	Helichrysum bracteatum	flower	air drying
sunflower	Helianthus	flower	air drying
sweet pea	Lathyrus odoratus	flower	desiccant
sweet William	Dianthus barbatus	flower	air dry quickly
tansy	Tanacetum vulgare	flower	air drying/ microwave
teasel	Dipsacus fullonum	seedhead	air drying
thistle	Carlina	seedhead	air drying
wheat (bearded)	Triticale	stems and seedheads	air drying
wheat (common)	Triticum aestiuum	stems and seedheads	air drying
tulip	Tulipa	flower	desiccant
vine	Vitus	leaf	desiccant
wallflower	Cheiranthus	flower	desiccant
winged spindle	Euonymus alatus	flower	air drying
xeranthemum (immortelle)	Xeranthemum	flower	air drying
yarrow	Achillea millefolium	flower	air drying
zinnia	Zinnia	flower	desiccant

CONTEMPORARY WREATHS

· · ·

MATERIALS

· · ·

*RED AND YELLOW
MATERIALS
scissors*

· · ·

34 red roses

· · ·

33 yellow roses

· · ·

florist's adhesive

· · ·

*plastic foam ring for dried
flowers, 10 cm (4 in) diameter*

· · ·

ribbon

· · ·

*BLUE AND WHITE
MATERIALS
scissors*

· · ·

25 white roses

· · ·

*26 small heads blue globe
thistle*

· · ·

glue

· · ·

*plastic foam ring for dried
flowers, 10 cm (4 in) diameter*

· · ·

ribbon

*The wreaths are simple to
make but will require a lot of
material and a little patience to
achieve the neat checker-board
patterns that characterize them.*

These two wall-hanging decorations show how massed dried flowers in strong contrasting colours can create a striking contemporary display.

One display couples white roses with blue globe thistles, the second red roses with yellow roses; but alternative materials can be used provided all the flower-heads used in any display are about the same size as each other. Consider using green *Nigella orientalis* with white roses, bleached white poppy seed heads with bright yellow helichrysums or blue sea holly with bright orange carthamus.

1 For the red and yellow wreath, cut the rose stems to 2.5 cm (1 in). Around the outside edge of the foam ring, form a circle of alternating yellow and red roses by gluing on their stems and pushing them into the foam. Leave a small gap in the rose circle for a ribbon. Inside the first circle, construct a second circle, offsetting the colours against the first ring.

2 Continue building circles of roses until the ring is covered. Pass the ribbon through the centre and around the gap on the plastic foam ring. Use the ribbon to hang the wreath or tie in a bow. Follow the same method for the second wreath.

Terracotta Plant-Pot Display

• • •

This delightful selection of dried flower arrangements in terracotta pots shows the exciting colours and types of flowers now available. Massed flowers in bright colours are presented in a contemporary way but in old-fashioned terracotta thumb (rose) pots, the rustic charm of which has been enhanced by colouring their surfaces.

The display will have the greatest impact when used as a group but you could place them individually around the rooms of your house if you prefer.

MATERIALS
. . .
1 block plastic foam for dried
flowers
. . .
knife
. . .
5 old-fashioned terracotta pots,
coloured with chalk
. . .
scissors
. . .
16 pink dried roses
. . .
7 dried sunflower heads
. . .
1 bunch dried lavender
. . .
25 small cinnamon sticks
. . .
10 stems Craspedia globosa
. . .
9 stems blue globe thistle

1 Cut the plastic foam for each pot and wedge it in so that it is about 2 cm (¾ in) below the rim. Cut all the stems so that when they are pushed into the plastic foam only their heads are visible above the rim of the pot. Fill one pot with tightly massed rose heads. In the second pot, push the sunflower heads into the plastic foam. Again, make sure that only the heads are visible above the rim of the pot. The aim is to achieve a massed domed effect in each pot.

Even the least experienced flower arranger will have no difficulty in creating these charming arrangements

2 Fill the third pot with lavender stems, cut so that the bottoms of the flower spikes are level with the rim of the pot. Break the cinnamon sticks to create jagged ends, making them about 10 cm (4 in) long. Push them into the foam of the fourth pot, with the tops slightly varying in height. Cut the *Craspedia* and the globe thistle stems so their heads will appear just above the rim of the pot. Fill the fifth pot by creating a regular pattern of blue globe thistle in a yellow carpet of *Craspedia*.

DECORATED POT DISPLAY
. . .

MATERIALS
. . .
knife
. . .
*1 block plastic foam for dried
flowers*
. . .
*hand-painted terracotta plant
pot*
. . .
florist's adhesive tape
. . .
.71 wires
. . .
reindeer moss
. . .
scissors
. . .
20 stems small globe thistles
. . .
20 bleached cane spirals
. . .
30 stems dried white roses

*The display is basically
massed dried flowers with the
addition of curly cane spirals to
add height and humour. It is
quick-and-easy to make and
would be a fun decoration for a
child's bedroom.*

This display is purely for fun. The container is a terracotta pot decorated with
a painted head against a bright blue background. You can decorate a terracotta pot with your own design and create a complementary floral display for it.

As a general rule, if the container is in any way elaborate, then the floral display
in it should be simple, but this display is deliberately flamboyant because it is
designed to represent hair growing out of the painted head.

1 Cut the block of plastic foam so that it
wedges into the decorated pot and
extends approximately 4 cm (1¾ in) above
the rim. Secure it in place with adhesive
tape. Make hairpin shapes from the .71
wire. Tuck reindeer moss between the
sides of the pot and the plastic foam and
push the wire hairpins through the moss
and into the foam to secure.

2 Cut the globe thistle stems to
approximately 10 cm (4 in) in length
and arrange them throughout the plastic
foam to create an even domed shape.

3 Cut the cane spirals to a length of
about 15 cm (6 in) and push their
stems into the plastic foam, distributing
them evenly throughout the globe thistles.

4 Cut the stems of the dried roses to
approximately 10 cm (4 in) in length
and arrange them evenly amongst the
other materials in the display.

APPLE AND LAVENDER TOPIARY TREE

. . .

MATERIALS

. . .

*terracotta pot, 15 cm (6 in)
diameter*

. . .

cellophane (plastic wrap)

. . .

sand

. . .

knife

. . .

*1 block plastic foam for dried
flowers*

. . .

glue

. . .

*1 piece preserved (dried) root
with two branches*

. . .

*2 plastic foam balls, 12 cm
(4¾ in) diameter*

. . .

60 slices preserved (dried) apple

. . .

.71 wires

. . .

150 stems natural phalaris

. . .

scissors

. . .

30 stems cream dried roses

. . .

50 stems Nigella orientalis

. . .

20 stems natural ti tree

. . .

150 stems dried lavender

. . .

*12 short stems preserved
(dried) eucalyptus*

Decorative trees are often referred to as topiary trees, and whether made from fresh or dried materials can be designed to match the colour scheme and image of any room.

This dried flower and fruit example has soft soothing colours: pale green phalaris and *Nigella orientalis,* dusty blue lavender, white ti tree, soft grey eucalyptus and the creamy tones of the dried roses and apple slices.

Topiary trees have a tendency to be top heavy, especially if they have more than one branch. To counterbalance this, make sure that the container is weighted with wet sand or, as a more permanent measure, plaster of Paris.

1 Line the terracotta pot with cellophane (plastic wrap) or polythene (plastic sheeting) and three-quarters fill it with wet sand. Cut the block of plastic foam to fit the pot, firmly wedge it in on top of the sand and level it with the rim of the pot.

2 Put a few drops of glue on the base of the piece of root. With its branches pointed upwards, push the root into the centre of the plastic foam in the terracotta pot. Apply a few drops of glue on to the top of the branches and push one of the plastic foam balls on to each branch.

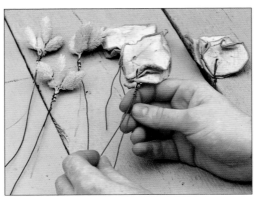

3 Form the apple slices into 20 groups of three. Push a .71 wire through the flesh of a group and bring the ends down, twisting together to form a double leg mount. Cut the phalaris stems to a length of about 3 cm (1¼ in) and form 30 groups of five, double leg mounting each group with .71 wire.

4 Cut the wires of the phalaris groups to approximately 4 cm (1½ in) and distribute them evenly all over the two balls by pushing the wired stems into the plastic foam. Cut the roses to a stem length of approximately 5 cm (2 in) and push the stems into the foam, distributing them evenly among the phalaris.

5 Cut the wire stems of the groups of apple slices to a length of approximately 4 cm (1½ in) and push them in to the foam, distributing them evenly around both balls. Cut 40 stems of the *Nigella orientalis* and all the stems of ti tree to a length of approximately 5 cm (2 in). Push the stems into the foam, distributing both evenly over the two balls.

6 Cut the lavender to an overall length of approximately 5 cm (2 in), form them in to 40 groups of three and push the stems of these groups into the foam. Position them evenly among the other materials on both balls.

7 Cut the eucalyptus stems and the remaining *Nigella orientalis* and lavender stems to varying lengths. At the base of the tree push these stems into the plastic foam to create an arrangement that covers the foam completely.

This tree is relatively intricate to make as it involves wiring and a large quantity of different materials. However, a more unusual effect can be achieved by the use of only one or two materials, for example the roses and the apple slices.

OLIVE-OIL CAN ROSE ARRANGEMENT

· · ·

· · ·

1 block plastic foam for dried flowers

· · ·

knife

· · ·

small rectangular olive oil can

· · ·

scissors

· · ·

40 stems dried 'Jacaranda' roses

· · ·

raffia

If you come across an eye-catching container, however unlikely, remember it may be just right for a floral display. And if you are using dried flowers it does not even need to be watertight.

An old olive oil can may not be the first thing to spring to mind when considering a container for your dried flower arrangement, but the bright reds, yellows and greens of this tin make it an attractive option.

Since this container is so striking, the arrangement is kept simple with only one type of flower and one colour used. This creates an effective contemporary display.

1 Cut the plastic foam to fit snugly in the olive oil can, filling it to 2 cm (¾ in) down from its rim.

2 Cut the dried roses so that they protrude about 10 cm (4 in) above the rim of the tin. Starting at the left-hand side of the tin, arrange a line of five tightly packed roses in the plastic foam from its front to its back. Continue arranging lines of five roses parallel to the first and closely packed to each other across the width of the tin.

3 Continue adding lines of roses until the roses are used up. Then take a small bundle of raffia about 3 cm (1¼ in) thick and twist it to make it compact. Loosely wrap the raffia round the stems of the roses just above the top of the tin and finish in a tied knot.

TIED PINK PEONY BOUQUET
· · ·

This lovely bouquet demonstrates how, by the use of modern preserving techniques, the strong natural colours of flowers can be retained after drying.

The spiralled bouquet is a loose, slightly domed arrangement that uses its flowers on long stems. The colours are extraordinarily rich for dried flowers, with deep pink roses and peonies and purple marjoram.

MATERIALS
· · ·
15 dried dark pink peonies
· · ·
30 dried dark pink roses
· · ·
1 bunch dried marjoram
· · ·
twine
· · ·
scissors
· · ·
ribbon

1 Lay all the materials in separate groups for easy access when working. Split the marjoram into 15 small bunches. Start building the bouquet by holding a dried peony in your hand about two-thirds the way down its stem. Add two stems of roses, then a small bunch of marjoram and another single peony, turning the bunch in your hand with every addition to make the stems form a spiral. Continue adding materials in this sequence, always turning the bunch in your hand to produce a spiral of stems. Occasionally vary your hand position to create a slightly domed shape.

As a gift, the bouquet would be a beautiful alternative to fresh flowers and since it is already arranged it can be put straight into a container.

2 When all the materials have been incorporated in the bunch, tie twine tightly around the binding point – the point where all the stems cross. Trim the stem ends so they are even and, below the binding point, make up about one-third of the overall height of the bouquet. Finally, tie a ribbon around the binding point and finish in a decorative bow.

31

SPICY STAR WALL DECORATION

· · ·

MATERIALS
· · ·
*15 cinnamon sticks, 30 cm
(12 in) long*
· · ·
raffia
· · ·
scissors
· · ·
75 lavender stems
· · ·
ribbon

*If a Christmas look is
required, substitute dried fruit
slices and gilded seed heads for
the lavender. Similarly, any
sturdy straight twigs can be
used instead of cinnamon.*

This star-shaped wall decoration is constructed from groups of long cinnamon sticks. It is embellished with bunches of lavender to add colour, texture, contrast and a scent which mixes with the warm, spicy smell of the cinnamon.

Its construction requires a bit of patience but is a simple matter of binding the materials together. Take care when handling the cinnamon as it can be brittle.

1 Separate the cinnamon sticks into five groups of three. Interlace the ends of two groups of sticks to form a point and secure firmly by tying them together with raffia. Trim the ends of the raffia.

2 Continue interlacing and binding together groups of cinnamon sticks to create a star-shaped framework. Also, bind together the sticks where they cross each other to make the frame rigid.

3 Separate the lavender into bunches of 15 stems each. Turn the star shape so that the binding knots are at the back and attach the bunches of lavender to the front of the frame, using raffia at the cross points of the cinnamon sticks.

4 When all the lavender bunches have been secured, make a small bow from the ribbon and tie it to the decoration at the bottom crossing point of the cinnamon sticks.

PEONY AND APPLE
TABLE ARRANGEMENT
· · ·

MATERIALS
· · ·
*1 block plastic foam for dried
flowers*
· · ·
knife
· · ·
terracotta bowl
· · ·
florist's adhesive tape
· · ·
scissors
· · ·
*10 stems preserved (dried)
eucalyptus*
· · ·
*18 slices preserved (dried)
apple*
· · ·
71 wires
· · ·
2 large heads dried hydrangea
· · ·
10 pale pink dried peonies
· · ·
20 deep pink dried roses
· · ·
20 dried peony leaves
· · ·
10 stems ti tree

This delicate arrangement can be made for a specific occasion and kept to be used again and again, whenever a special decoration is called for.

The construction of the decoration is relatively simple, involving the minimum of wiring.

1 Cut the block of plastic foam so that it wedges into the bowl and hold it securely in place with the florist's adhesive tape. Cut the eucalyptus stems to about 13 cm (5 in), making sure that the cut ends are clean of leaves, and arrange them evenly around the plastic foam to create a domed foliage outline to the display.

2 Group the slices of preserved (dried) apple into threes and double leg mount them with .71 wires. Push the six groups of wired apple slices into the foam, distributing them evenly throughout the display. The apple slices should be a little shorter than the eucalyptus when in place.

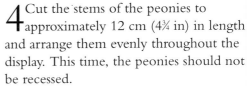

3 Break each hydrangea head into three smaller florets and push them into the foam, distributing them evenly throughout the display, and recessing them slightly as you work.

4 Cut the stems of the peonies to approximately 12 cm (4¾ in) in length and arrange them evenly throughout the display. This time, the peonies should not be recessed.

This pretty arrangement is suitable for a small table.

5 Cut the dried rose stems to approximately 13 cm (4¾ in) in length and push them into the plastic foam throughout the other materials in the arrangement.

6 Arrange the dried peony leaves evenly amongst the flowers. Cut the ti tree into stems of approximately 13 cm (4¾ in) in length and distribute them throughout the display.

ROSE AND STARFISH WREATH
. . .

MATERIALS
. . .
10 small dried starfish
. . .
.71 wires
. . .
scissors
. . .
florist's adhesive
. . .
*plastic foam ring for dried
flowers, 13 cm (5 in) diameter*
. . .
45 shell-pink dried rose heads
. . .
velvet ribbon

*The construction of this
wreath involves a small
amount of wiring, but is
otherwise straightforward.*

The design of this visually simple wall decoration involves massing a single type of flower and framing them with a halo of geometric shapes, in this case stars. The prettiness of its soft peach colours makes it suitable for a bedroom wall, in which case sprinkle it with scented oil.

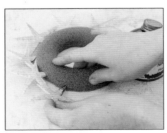

1 Double leg mount the starfish as an extension of one of their arms with a .71 wire. Cut the wire to about 2.5 cm (1 in) and apply florist's adhesive to both the tip of the starfish arm and wire. Push the wired arm into the outside edge of the plastic foam ring. Position all the starfish around the ring. Leave a gap of 3 cm (1¼ in) for attaching the ribbon.

2 Cut the stems of the rose heads to about 2.5 cm (1 in) and put florist's adhesive on their stems and bases. Push the glued stems into the plastic foam to form a ring around its outside edge on top of the starfish. Working towards the centre of the ring, continue forming circles of rose heads until the ring is covered apart from a gap for the ribbon.

3 Pass the ribbon through the centre of the ring and position it so that it sits in the gap between the roses and starfish to cover the foam. This can be used to hang up the wreath or just tied in a bow for decoration.

PEONY AND SHELL DISPLAY

· · ·

This display cleverly mixes sea shells with flowers in a lovely pink, mauve and green arrangement. The result is a beautiful compact dome. The main feature of the display is the beautifully patterned rose-pink conical sea shells which are echoed by the colour and texture of the cracked glazed ceramic container.

MATERIALS

· · ·

knife

· · ·

*1 block plastic foam for dried
flowers*

· · ·

ceramic bowl

· · ·

florist's adhesive tape

· · ·

scissors

· · ·

*12 stems dried pale pink
peonies*

· · ·

3 dried heads hydrangea

· · ·

7 pink conical shells

This arrangement would be perfect for a bathroom, as long as it is not allowed to become too damp.

1 Cut the plastic foam so that it fits snugly into the container and secure it in place with the florist's adhesive tape. Strip the leaves from the peony stems and cut the stems to about 9 cm (3½ in) long. Push the stems into the foam to create a regular dome shape. Arrange the peony leaves liberally throughout the display.

2 Break each hydrangea head into three clusters and push them into the foam, distributing them among the peony heads. Distribute the sea shells throughout the display by pushing their wider bottom ends between the flowers so that they are held in place by the mass of blooms (secure with glue if necessary).

SUMMER DISPLAYS

· · ·

MATERIALS

· · ·

10 stems dried purple larkspur

· · ·

2 pitchers

· · ·

10 stems dried pink larkspur

· · ·

*10 stems blue globe thistle
(small heads)*

· · ·

*10 stems dried green
amaranthus (straight)*

· · ·

*16 stems dried deep pink
peonies*

· · ·

scissors

*Use the displays in a pair to
achieve the maximum impact.*

The majority of people buying fresh summer cut flowers would think of doing no more than informally arranging them in a vase or pitcher of water. These two matching displays in similar pitchers are loosely arranged in what is almost the dried flower equivalent of this informal approach to flower arranging.

The two displays are characterized by their use of summer flowers in typical summer colours: purple and pink larkspur, blue globe thistle, deep pink peonies and green amaranthus.

Creating the displays requires only the most relaxed approach to dried-flower arranging – you just need to consider carefully the visual balance of the materials to their containers.

1 Split the materials into two equal groups. Cut the purple larkspur so that the stems are approximately three times the height of pitchers. Arrange five stems of purple larkspur loosely in each pitcher. Cut the stems of the pink larkspur to a similar length to the purple larkspur.

2 Arrange the pink larkspur in each pitcher. Break off any offshoots on the globe thistle stems to use separately. Cut the main globe thistle stems to three times the height of the pitchers and arrange in each. Separate the offshoots of globe thistle and arrange in each pitcher.

3 Cut the stems of amaranthus to three times the height of the pitchers and arrange five stems in each.

4 Cut the peony stems to different heights, the tallest being 2.5 cm (1 in) shorter than the larkspur, and the shortest being 20 cm (8 in) shorter than the larkspur. Arrange the peonies evenly throughout the other materials.

ROSE AND LEMON NOSEGAY

• • •

MATERIALS

• • •

*3 dried lemons with splits in
their skin*

• • •

.71 wires

• • •

scissors

• • •

15 stems globe thistles

• • •

15 stems dried yellow roses

• • •

twine

• • •

ribbon

*Although the lemons have to
be wired, this is a simple
decoration to make.*

Traditionally a nosegay was a small tight bunch of selected herbs, sometimes with flowers, carried about the person, the scent of which was used to combat bad odours and protect against disease. Effectively it was portable pot-pourri. Today the content of a nosegay is just as likely to be chosen for its appearance as its strong aroma.

This nosegay has whole dried lemons, yellow dried roses and blue globe thistles, and is finished with a ribbon tied in a bow. While the roses and lemons have a faint scent, this can be augmented either by steeping the ribbon in cologne or by sprinkling the materials with perfumed oils.

1 Wire the dried lemons by pushing a .71 wire into a split near the base, through the lemon and out of a split on its other side. Bend the wires downwards and twist the two pieces together under the bases of the lemons.

2 Cut the globe thistle and rose stems to approximately 12 cm (4½ in). Start with a dried rose as the central flower and build a small spiralled posy around it by evenly adding the other ingredients.

3 When all the materials have been formed into a tight round posy, tie it with twine at the binding point. Trim the bottom of the stems. Make a ribbon bow and attach it to the binding point.

FLOWER CONE

· · ·

This unusual design employs a series of stacked rings around a cone shape, each ring containing massed flowers of one type and colour to create a quirky display with a strong geometric pattern.

One side of the container is higher than the other so its rim is an ellipse rather than a circle and this is exploited by making the rings of the flowers follow this elliptical shape to form lines of colour sweeping down from back to front.

MATERIALS
· · ·
plastic foam cone for dried flowers, 28 cm (11 in) high
· · ·
galvanized metal container, approximately 11 cm (4½ in) diameter
· · ·
scissors
· · ·
20 stems dried floss flower
· · ·
40 stems dried pink rose heads
· · ·
20 stems dried marjoram
· · ·
10 stems small dried globe thistle heads
· · ·
ribbon

1 Wedge the plastic foam cone firmly into the galvanized container. Cut the floss flower stems to about 2.5 cm (1 in) long and arrange a ring around the bottom of the cone to follow the ellipse of the rim of the container. Cut the rose stems to about 2.5 cm (1 in) long and, tight to the first ring, arrange a second ring with the rose heads again following the elliptical shape.

The pretty colours of the display and finishing ribbon make it ideal for a dressing-table where a mirror at its back will show the arrangement in the round.

2 Cut the stems of the marjoram and globe thistle to about 2.5 cm (1 in). Tight to the ring of rose heads, form a third elliptical ring with the marjoram. Tight to the marjoram, form a fourth elliptical ring with the globe thistle. Repeat this sequence of rings until all the cone is covered. At the tip, fix a single rose head.

3 Wrap the ribbon around the galvanized metal container and finish it in a small tied bow at the front of the display.

41

MATERIALS

. . .

knife

. . .

1 block plastic foam for dried flowers

. . .

small basket, approximately 12.5 cm (5 in) diameter

. . .

florist's adhesive tape

. . .

scissors

. . .

5 stems natural dried honesty

. . .

20 stems dried spray roses

. . .

50 stems natural dried phalaris heads

. . .

ribbon

This delicate and pretty little display is designed as a centrepiece for a table laden with summer foods – and whether your dinner party is inside or outside, this display is perfect.

The materials in the arrangement, peach-pink spray roses and pale green honesty and phalaris, combine to create a soufflé of summer colours. Enhance its seasonal feel by sprinkling it with summer scented oil.

1 Cut the plastic foam to fit the basket, so that it projects 2 cm (¾ in) above its rim, and tape it into place using florist's adhesive tape.

2 Take a stem of honesty and cut off the small offshoots of dried seed heads. Use these seed heads on stems cut to about 8 cm (3¼ in), to create a foliage outline.

3 Cut the dried spray roses to a stem length of approximately 8 cm (3¼ in) and arrange them evenly and densely in the plastic foam throughout the honesty.

*A*ll the materials have
relatively fragile stems which
require careful handling,
especially when pushing them
into the plastic foam.

4 Cut the phalaris stems to a length of
about 8 cm (3¼ in) and distribute
them evenly throughout the honesty and
spray roses.

5 Once all the materials have been used
up, tie the ribbon around the basket,
finishing it in a bow at the front.

MASSED ARRANGEMENT IN BLUE AND YELLOW

· · ·

MATERIALS

· · ·

*1 galvanized shallow bucket,
30 cm (12 in) diameter*

· · ·

*2 blocks plastic foam for dried
flowers*

· · ·

florist's adhesive tape

· · ·

scissors

· · ·

*25 large dyed blue globe thistle
heads*

· · ·

*35 dried natural heads yellow
achillea*

*This table decoration would
complement a modern kitchen
or dining-room.*

This contemporary arrangement uses simple massed materials in strong contrasting colours to achieve a strikingly bold display. The polished texture of the silver-grey galvanized bucket provides an ideal visual foundation on which to build the domed cushion of deep yellow achillea with contrasting spiky, blue globe thistles.

No special techniques are required to construct the display but you must ensure the materials are massed to achieve the surface density necessary.

1 Wedge the blocks of foam in place and tape. Cut the globe thistle stems to around 12 cm (4¼ in) and arrange in the foam. Use smaller heads around the outside and larger heads at the centre.

2 Cut the achillea stems to about 12 cm (4¾ in) and arrange them between the globe thistles, massing them carefully so that no gaps are visible.

GLOBE THISTLE AND MUSSEL SHELL RING

・ ・ ・

I f you were wondering what to do with all those shells you collected during last year's seaside holiday, this decoration may be the answer. The material content of this display is strongly evocative of the seaside. The spiky globe thistles contrast with the smooth hard surface of the mussel shells, but probably the most memorable feature of the display is its beautiful blue colouring.

MATERIALS

・ ・ ・

plastic foam ring for dried flowers, 13 cm (5 in) diameter

・ ・ ・

glue gun and glue

・ ・ ・

9 half mussel shells

・ ・ ・

65 globe thistle heads of various sizes

・ ・ ・

scissors

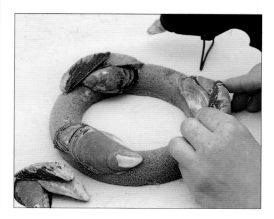

T he ring would look wonderful displayed in either a bathroom or a kitchen.

1 Position groups of three slightly overlapping mussel shells at three equidistant points around the ring. Glue them to the plastic foam and to each other, taking great care when using the glue gun which will be very hot.

2 Cut the globe thistle stems to around 2.5 cm (1 in) long, put a small blob of glue on the stem and push them into the plastic foam. Continue this process until all areas of the plastic foam not covered with shells are filled.

SUMMER HAT FRUIT DECORATION

. . .

MATERIALS

. . .

30 dried orange slices

. . .

.71 wires

. . .

30 dried lemon slices

. . .

30 dried apple slices

. . .

florist's tape (stem-wrap tape)

. . .

scissors

. . .

10 dried sunflowers

. . .

straw hat

. . .

.32 silver reel (rose) wire

To avoid an embarrassing encounter with someone wearing the same hat as you at that wedding or day at the races, create your own unique headwear.

By the addition of the bright summery colours of dried sunflowers, and orange and lemon slices, a plain straw hat is transformed into a millinery masterpiece.

1 Divide the orange slices into groups of three and double leg mount each group on .71 wire. Repeat the process for the lemon and apple slices. Cover the wired stems with florist's tape (stem-wrap tape). Cut the stems of the sunflowers to 2.5 cm (1 in). Double leg mount on .71 wire and cover the wired stems with the tape.

2 Construct a stay wire by grouping together four .71 wires, each overlapping the next by about 3 cm (1¼ in), and taping them together with florist's tape (stem-wrap tape). Continue adding wires until you have reached the required length – approximately 4 cm (1¾ in) longer than the circumference of the crown of the hat.

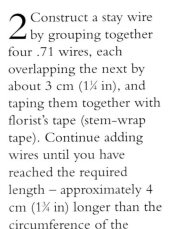

3 Arrange your wired materials into separate groups for easy access while you work. Tape the individual wired materials on to the stay wire in the following repeating sequence: orange slices; apple slices; sunflower heads and lemon slices. Continue this along the whole length of the stay wire bending it into the shape of the crown of the hat as you work and leaving the last 4 cm (1¾ in) undecorated. Take the undecorated end of the stay wire and tape it to the other end through the flowers.

4 Place the completed garland over the crown of the hat so that it sits on the brim, and stitch in position by pushing lengths of .32 reel (rose) wire through the straw and around the stay wire at four equidistant positions around the hat. Once in position, you may want to adjust the wired elements to achieve the best effect.

The hat decoration is similar to a garland headdress and its construction, although involving wiring, is relatively straightforward.

STARFISH AND ROSE TABLE DECORATION

· · ·

MATERIALS

· · ·

9 small dried starfish

· · ·

.71 wires

· · ·

*church candle, 7.5 x 22.5 cm
(5 x 9 in)*

· · ·

*plastic foam ring for dried
flowers, 7.5 cm (3 in) diameter*

· · ·

scissors

· · ·

reindeer moss

· · ·

40 dried rose heads

*The cream roses complement
the colour of the candle and
contrast is provided by the
apricot colour and strong
geometric shape of the small
dried starfish.*

This is an alternative decoration for a large church candle using dried rose heads and starfish. The result is a table centre decoration with a seaside feel. This is a simple and quick decoration to make, but is very effective nonetheless.

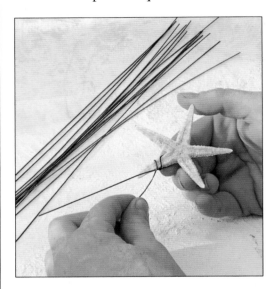

1 Double leg mount all the starfish individually through one arm with .71 wires to extend their overall length. Cut the wires to approximately 2.5 cm (1 in) in length and put to one side.

2 Position the candle in the centre of the plastic foam ring. Make 2 cm (1¾ in) long hairpins from cut lengths of .71 wires. Use these to pin the reindeer moss around the edge of the ring.

3 Group the wired starfish into sets of three and position each group equidistant from the others around the foam ring. Push their wires into the foam to secure.

4 Cut the stems of the dried rose heads to about 2.5 cm (1 in) and push the stems into the foam to form two continuous tightly packed rings of flowers around the candle.

ARTICHOKE PINHOLDER
DISPLAY
• • •

MATERIALS

• • •

pedestal stand

• • •

1 pinholder

• • •

scissors

• • •

6 stems contorted hazel

• • •

9 stems dried artichoke heads

• • •

*25 stems dried poppy seed
heads*

*Use naturally trailing stems of
hazel at the front of the
pinholder and bring it down
over the pedestal to the right of
its centre line to create a
natural trailing effect.*

This otherwise traditional line arrangement is unusual in that dried materials are used on a pinholder. Dried stems are hard and it is not easy to push them on to the spikes of a pinholder. There is also the heaviness of the artichokes to consider and they have to be carefully positioned to avoid disrupting the physical balance of the arrangement. Make sure that all the stems are firmly pushed on to the pinholder's spikes.

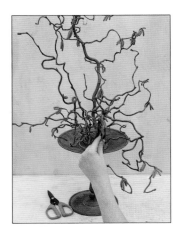

1 Push the hazel stems, cut to 45 cm (18 in) on to the spikes of the pinholder, positioning the tallest stem at the back.

2 Arrange the artichoke heads throughout the hazel. Use the smallest head on the longest stem centrally at the back. Work away from this with progressively shorter stems. Position the largest artichoke head about two-thirds down from the top of the display.

3 Arrange the poppy seed head stems throughout the display. Position the longest stem at the back, making sure it is shorter than the tallest hazel stem but taller than the tallest artichoke. Work away from this point with progressively shorter stems, with some stems trailing over the front to the right of centre.

SMALL CANDLEHOLDER DISPLAY

• • •

There are many containers in the average household which, because of their colour, shape or material content, are suitable for a flower arrangement. This display was inspired entirely by the small crown-shaped, brass candleholder in which it is arranged.

An elevated position on, for example, a mantelpiece, would be perfect for such a small, neat display. Indeed, it could be used as a wedding-cake decoration.

MATERIALS

• • •

knife

• • •

1 block plastic foam for dried flowers

• • •

crown-shaped candleholder

• • •

scissors

• • •

15 stems poppy seed heads

• • •

20 stems dried pink roses

1 Cut a piece of plastic foam so that it can be wedged firmly into the candle holder, and sits about 2 cm (¾ in) below its top edge.

2 Cut the stems of the poppy seed heads to 9 cm (3½ in) and push them into the foam, distributing them evenly to create a domed shape.

3 Cut the dried rose stems to 9 cm (3½ in) and push them into the foam between the poppy seed heads, to reinforce the domed outline.

Making the display is straightforward and the method is applicable to any arrangement in a similarly small container.

EDGING BASKET
IN BLUE
· · ·

MATERIALS
· · ·

scissors

· · ·

33 stems globe thistle

· · ·

.71 wires

· · ·

24 stems sea holly

· · ·

.38 silver wire

· · ·

1 bunch floss flower

· · ·

1 bunch marjoram

· · ·

60 stems lavender

· · ·

florist's tape (stem-wrap tape)

· · ·

.32 silver reel (rose) wire

· · ·

*wire-mesh and rectangular
cane basket*

*Dried flowers transform the
basket into an attractive object
you would happily put on
display in your house.*

Tired household containers can be decorated to give them a new lease of life. This might simply be a fresh coat of paint or, as in the case of this wire mesh and cane basket, a dried-flower edging around its rim.

The display uses the blues and mauves of marjoram, floss flower, lavender, globe thistle and sea holly to create a decoration with memorable colour and texture.

1 Cut the globe thistle stems to 2.5 cm (1 in) long and double leg mount each with .71 wire. Cut the sea holly stems to 2.5 cm (1 in) and double leg mount each with .38 silver wire. Split the floss flower and the marjoram into 20 small clusters of each on stems 5 cm (2 in) long and double leg mount them individually with .38 silver wire. Cut the lavender stems to about 5 cm (2 in) long, group in threes and double leg mount each group with .38 silver wire. Cover all the wired elements with florist's tape (stem-wrap tape).

2 Lay a wired stem of sea holly on the edge of the basket and attach it by binding it in place with a length of .32 silver reel (rose) wire. Slightly overlap the sea holly with a cluster of floss flower, binding in place with .32 silver reel (rose) wire. Overlap the floss flower with a globe thistle head, the globe thistle with the marjoram and the marjoram with the lavender, binding all of them firmly to the basket with the same continuous length of reel wire. Repeat the sequence of materials all around the edge of the basket. When the entire edge of the basket is covered, stitch the reel wire through the basket several times to secure.

PEONIES AND ARTICHOKES
IN AN URN
• • •

knife

• • •

*1 block plastic foam for dried
flowers*

• • •

small cast-iron urn

• • •

florist's adhesive tape

• • •

scissors

• • •

*5 stems dried heads of
flowering artichoke*

• • •

*8 stems dried pale pink
peonies*

• • •

*16 stems dried poppy seed
heads*

*The aim of this arrangement
is to show off the attractive
container, so the normal rules
of proportion have been turned
on their head: the vase
accounts for two-thirds of this
arrangement.*

Some containers merit an arrangement specifically designed to show them off and in order to do this, the floral display should neither be too high nor too wide and certainly should not trail down over it.

The particular attraction of this small cast-iron urn is its tall, elegant outline and the grey bloom of its surface. To make the most of the container, the arrangement has been kept low and compact in low-key colours. Pale pink peonies and brown artichokes with purple tufts are set against poppy seedheads with a grey bloom to match the urn.

1 Cut the block of plastic foam so that it can be wedged into the urn level with the rim. Secure the foam in place using florist's adhesive tape.

2 Cut the artichoke stems to about 13 cm (5¼ in). Push one stem into the foam at its centre. Position the other stems around the central stem by pushing them into the foam so that they are slightly shorter, creating a domed outline.

3 Cut the peony stems to about 13 cm (5¼ in) long and push them into the foam evenly and tightly massed throughout but slightly recessed below the artichoke heads.

4 Cut the poppy stems to about 13 cm (5¼ in) long and push them into the plastic foam evenly throughout the artichokes and peonies with their heads level with the artichoke heads.

PEONY AND GLOBE THISTLE
CANDLE DECORATION
· · ·

MATERIALS
· · ·
knife
· · ·
*block of plastic foam for dried
flowers*
· · ·
*terracotta pot, 15 cm (6 in)
diameter*
· · ·
wide candle
· · ·
10 dried deep pink peonies
· · ·
*15 stems dried small blue globe
thistle*
· · ·
scissors

*The effect of this display relies
on the peonies being tightly
massed together. Never leave
burning candles unattended
and do not allow the candles to
burn beclow 5 cm (2 in) of the
display.*

This beautiful arrangement of dried flowers in a terracotta pot is designed to incorporate a candle. Contemporary in its use of massed flowerheads, the display has the stunning colour combination of deep pink peonies and bright blue globe thistles surrounding a dark green candle and finished with a lime-green ribbon. It would make a wonderful gift.

Simple to construct, you could make several arrangements, using different colours and display them as a group. Alternatively, you could change the scale by using a larger container, more flowers and incorporating more than one candle.

1 Cut a piece of plastic foam to size and wedge it firmly into the terracotta pot. Push the candle into the centre of the plastic foam so that it is held securely and sits upright.

2 Cut the peony stems to 4 cm (1½ in) and the globe thistle stems to 5 cm (2 in). Push the stems of the peonies into the foam. Push the stems of the globe thistle into the foam amongst the peonies.

3 Ensure that the heads of all the flowers are at the same level. Wrap a ribbon around the top of the terracotta pot and tie it in a bow at the front. Shape the ends of the ribbon to avoid fraying.

SUMMER POT-POURRI
· · ·

The traditional pot-pourri is based on rose petals because when fresh they have a powerful fragrance, some of which is retained when they are dried, unlike many other perfumed flowers. Today's pot-pourri does not rely entirely on the fragrance of its flowers since there is a wide range of scented oils available and this means materials can be used just for their visual qualities.

This pot-pourri is traditional in that it uses dried roses, but modern in that whole buds and heads have been included instead of petals. The sea holly heads, apple slices and whole lemons are used entirely for their appearance.

MATERIALS
· · ·
20 stems lavender
· · ·
*15 preserved (dried) apple
slices*
· · ·
5 dried lemons
· · ·
1 handful cloves
· · ·
20 dried pale pink rose heads
· · ·
2 handfuls dried rose buds
· · ·
1 handful hibiscus buds
· · ·
10 sea holly heads
· · ·
large glass bowl
· · ·
pot-pourri essence
· · ·
tablespoon

1 Break the stems off the lavender leaving only the flower spikes. Place all the dried ingredients in the glass bowl and mix together thoroughly. Add several drops of pot-pourri essence to the mixture of materials – the more you add the stronger the scent. Stir thoroughly to mix the scent throughout the pot-pourri, using a spoon. As the perfume weakens with time it can be topped up by the addition of more drops of essence.

Predominantly pink and purple, the look and scent of this pot-pourri will enhance any home throughout the summer months.

BATHROOM DISPLAY

· · ·

MATERIALS

· · ·

2 blocks plastic foam for dried flowers

· · ·

knife

· · ·

pale-coloured wooden trug

· · ·

florist's adhesive tape

· · ·

scissors

· · ·

50 stems natural phalaris

· · ·

40 stems shell-pink roses

· · ·

20 stems cream-coloured helichrysums

· · ·

150 stems dried lavender

· · ·

15 small dried starfish

· · ·

.71 wires

Though a steamy environment will cause dried flowers to deteriorate, if you accept the shorter life span, such arrangements are an opportunity to add an attractive decorative feature to a bathroom. The starfish in this arrangement evoke images of the sea, whilst the soft pastel colours – shell-pink, apricot, blue, pale green and cream – give it a soft summer look.

Oval shaped, in a rectangular wooden trug, the display is a traditional full arrangement which can be viewed in the round and used anywhere in the house where its pastel shades would look appropriate. The scale and colour of the arrangement is designed to show off the faded blue container.

1 Cut the block of plastic foam to fit the wooden trug and secure it in place with adhesive tape. Cut the individual stems of phalaris to a length of approximately 10 cm (4 in) and push them into the plastic foam to establish the height, width and overall shape of the arrangement.

2 Cut the stems of the dried roses to a length of approximately 10 cm (4 in) and push them into the plastic foam, distributing them evenly throughout.

3 Cut the stems of the helichrysum to a length of about 10 cm (4 in) and push them into the foam amongst the roses and phalaris, recessing some. Cut the dried lavender to 11 cm (4½ in) and, by pushing into the foam, arrange it throughout the display in groups of five stems.

4 Wire all the starfish individually by double leg mounting one of the arms with a .71 wire. Cut the wire legs of the starfish to a length of about 10 cm (4 in) and push the wires into the foam, distributing them evenly throughout the display.

This display involves some wiring but the even distribution of materials helps make it simple to build.

DIAMOND, HEART, SPADE AND CLUB WREATHS

· · ·

These light-hearted wall decorations are instantly recognizable and would make a strong display either grouped together, perhaps in a line, or even individually framed and used separately.

Each decoration uses a single type of material in one colour and has its own distinctive texture. This reinforces the shape of each wreath. The diamond decoration has scented blue lavender spires used directionally to emphasize its simple shape. Appropriately, the heart display incorporates papery-textured red roses. The outline of the spade is formed from pale brown, oval poppy seed heads with distinctive star-shaped crowns and a lovely grey bloom. And bulbous, ribbed nigella seed heads in pale green and burgundy stripes define the shape of the club wreath.

Quite apart from any other consideration, making these decorations is an excellent exercise in taping and wiring techniques. It teaches valuable lessons about the versatility of stay wires in achieving relatively complex shapes, and how the choice of material affects the form of a floral decoration. Begin with the diamond, the simplest of the shapes, and work through the progressively more complex sequence of heart, spade and club and you will encounter an increasing number of factors to take into account to achieve a successful display. It is particularly important to grade the size of materials for both practical considerations, such as decorating difficult corners, and to emphasize features of outline shape.

Making these decorations will increase your understanding and experience of flower arranging and at the same time you will have created unusual and attractive displays.

LAVENDER DIAMOND WREATH

· · ·

1 Make a stay wire from .71 wire on which the decoration can be built. Cover with florist's tape (stem-wrap tape). Form the stay wire into a diamond shape about 22 cm (8¾ in) high with the two ends meeting at the bottom point.

MATERIALS

· · ·

.71 wires

· · ·

florist's tape (stem-wrap tape)

· · ·

scissors

· · ·

105 stems dried lavender

· · ·

.38 silver wires

*E*nsure that all the lavender spires point in the same direction to give this simple wreath maximum impact.

2 Cut the lavender to an overall length of approximately 5 cm (2 in) and group it in threes. Double leg mount these groups with .38 wires, then tape the 35 wired groups with florist's tape (stem–wrap tape).

3 Start at the top point of the diamond shape and attach the groups of lavender by taping around their wired stems and the stay wire. Slightly overlap one group with the next to achieve a continuous line around one half of the shape, finishing at the bottom open end of the stay wire. Start covering the second half of the diamond shape from the bottom open end of the stay wire. When covered, tape the two open ends together.

NIGELLA CLUB WREATH
· · ·

.71 wires

· · ·

florist's tape (stem-wrap tape)

· · ·

scissors

· · ·

*57 stems dried nigella seed
heads of similar size*

· · ·

.38 silver wires

*This wreath makes an eye-
catching and fun decoration.*

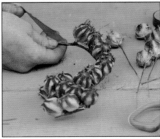

1 Make a stay wire from .71 wire on which the decoration can be built. Cover with florist's tape (stem-wrap tape). Form the stay wire into a club shape about 22 cm (8¾ in) high with the two ends of the wire meeting in a line at the centre at the bottom of the shape.

2 Cut the stems of the nigella to a length of approximately 2.5 cm (1 in) and double leg mount the individual nigella seedheads on .38 silver wires. Tape the wired stems with florist's tape (stem-wrap tape).

3 Starting at the beginning of the stay wire, tape the wired heads of nigella to the stay wire. Slightly overlap the nigella heads to achieve a continuous line. Continue until the stay wire is covered and then join the two ends of the wire together by taping.

ROSE HEART WREATH

· · ·

MATERIALS

· · ·

.71 wires

· · ·

florist's tape (stem-wrap tape)

· · ·

scissors

· · ·

50 stems dried red roses

· · ·

.38 silver wires

This effective heart would make an unusual and long-lasting Valentine's day gift.

  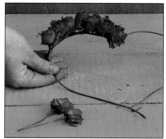

1 Make a stay wire from .71 wire on which the decoration can be built. Cover with florist's tape (stem-wrap tape). Form the stay wire into a heart shape about 22 cm (8¾ in) high with the two ends of the wire meeting at its bottom point.

2 Cut the stems of the dried roses to a length of approximately 2.5 cm (1 in) and double leg mount them individually on .38 silver wires, then tape the wired stems with florist's tape (stem-wrap tape) to hide the wire.

3 Starting at the top, tape the rose stems to the stay wire. Slightly overlap the roses to achieve a continuous line of heads, finishing at its bottom point. Starting back at the top, repeat the process around the other half of the heart. Tape the two ends of the wire together.

POPPY SPADE WREATH

· · ·

MATERIALS

· · ·

.71 wires

· · ·

florist's tape (stem-wrap tape)

· · ·

scissors

· · ·

*50 stems dried poppy seed
heads*

· · ·

.38 silver wires

*It is important to tape the
poppy seed heads closely
together so that they can rest
against each other and not
"flop" down.*

1 Make a stay wire from .71 wire on
which the decoration can be built.
Cover with florist's tape (stem-wrap tape).
Form the stay wire into a spade shape
about 22 cm (8¾ in) high with the two
ends of the wire meeting in a line at the
bottom of the shape.

2 Cut the stems of the poppy seed heads
to a length of approximately 2.5 cm
(1 in) and double leg mount the
individual poppy seed heads on .38 silver
wires, then tape the wired stems with
florist's tape (stem-wrap tape) to hide
the wire.

3 Starting at the pointed
top of the shape, tape
the poppy seed heads to
the stay wire starting with
the smallest. Slightly
overlap the seed heads to
achieve a continuous line.
The size of the heads
should be increased as you
work towards the bulbous
part of the shape, after
which the heads should be
decreased. When you have
completed one side, repeat
the whole process on the
opposite side, again
starting from the point at
the top. Tape the two ends
of the stay wire together
with tape.

WINTER POT-POURRI
· · ·

The concept of a pot-pourri probably dates from the Elizabethan period when they were used to produce a fragrance to combat the all-pervading bad smells of the times.

This pot-pourri uses its material content in substantial forms – whole oranges, pomegranates, sunflower heads and rose heads with big pieces of cinnamon – because they are included for how they look, not how they smell.

The pot-pourri is mixed using ready-dried materials and although the cloves and cinnamon give it some added spice, it is also worth adding spicy scented oils. A final dusting with gold dust powder gives it a festive Christmas look.

MATERIALS
· · ·
1 handful cloves
· · ·
1 handful dried hibiscus buds
· · ·
1 handful dried tulip petals
· · ·
1 handful small cones
· · ·
7 dried oranges
· · ·
5 dried sunflower heads
· · ·
1 handful dried red rose heads
· · ·
5 small dried pomegranates
· · ·
10 dried grapefruit slices
· · ·
10 cinnamon sticks
· · ·
large glass bowl
· · ·
pot-pourri spicy essence
· · ·
gold dust powder
· · ·
tablespoon

*T*his pot-pourri is very easy to make, so why not have several large bowls of it around the house in winter?

1 Place all the dried ingredients except the cinnamon in the glass bowl and mix together thoroughly. Break the cinnamon sticks into large pieces and add to the mixture.

2 Add several drops of the essence to the mixture. Scatter a tablespoon of gold dust powder over the mixture and stir it well to distribute the gold dust powder and essence throughout the pot-pourri.

EXOTIC ARRANGEMENT
. . .

*1 block plastic foam for dried
flowers*

. . .

knife

. . .

small cast-iron urn

. . .

florist's adhesive tape

. . .

scissors

. . .

.71 wires

. . .

handful reindeer moss

. . .

1 branch contorted willow

. . .

10 stems Protea compacta
buds

. . .

15 stems small pink
Protea compacta

. . .

3 stems Banksia hookerana

. . .

3 bean stems

. . .

3 stems Banksia coccinea

*T*ake care when building the
arrangement because the stems
are hard and will damage the
plastic foam if pushed in and
pulled out too often.

*T*his display is designed to produce an interesting counterpoint between the unusual floral materials and the traditional way in which they are arranged in a classic cast-iron urn. The rusting surface of the container beautifully complements the brown, pink and orange colouring of the materials.

The forms and textures of the individual contents of the arrangement are strong and hard but the overall effect is softened by the delicate twisting stems of contorted willow which work with the rest of the materials to create harmony within the display.

1 Cut the plastic foam to fit neatly into the urn with a 6.5 cm (2¾ in) projection above its rim. Secure it in place with florist's adhesive tape.

2 Make hairpins from the .71 wires and pin the reindeer moss to the plastic foam around the rim of the urn so that it tumbles over its edge.

3 Establish the overall height, width and fan shape of the arrangement with stems of contorted willow pushed into the plastic foam.

4 Arrange the *Protea compacta* amongst the willow, with the tallest at the back and shorter stems towards the sides and front. Position the *Banksia hookerana* stems in the same way, starting with the tallest at the back.

5 Position the dried bean stems adjacent to the *Banksia hookerana,* reducing their height towards the front. Place the *Banksia coccinea* stems evenly through the display at varying heights.

6 Push the stems of the *Protea compacta* buds into the foam, evenly arranging them throughout the display and decreasing their height from the back to the front and sides.

TEXTURED FOLIAGE RING

· · ·

*Very easy to construct from
commercially available
materials, this foliage ring
makes a wonderful autumn
wall decoration for a hall or, if
protected from the weather, a
front door.*

S ome types of foliage can be successfully air dried but many others cannot and
need to be glycerine preserved.

This decoration mixes both types of foliage to create a feast of textures and
subtle colours that succeeds without the enhancement of flowers.

1 Cut all the foliage stems to around 12 cm (4¾ in) long. You will need 21 lengths of each type of foliage to cover your ring. Start by securely tying a group of three stems of honesty to the wicker ring with twine.

2 Making sure it slightly overlaps the honesty, bind on a group of three glycerined beech stems with the same continuous length of twine. Repeat this process with a group of three stems of hops followed by a group of three stems of glycerined adiantum.

3 Continue binding materials to the ring in the same sequence until the ring is completely covered. Cut off any untidy stems and adjust the materials to achieve the best effect if necessary. Finally, tie off the twine in a discreet knot at the back of the ring.

WALL HANGING SHEAF

· · ·

The rustic charm of this delightful hand-tied sheaf is difficult to resist especially since it is so easy to make once you have mastered the ever-useful stem-spiralling technique.

The focal flowers are large, round, orange globe thistle heads, the hard, spiky geometry of which is set against the creamy-white papery flowers of the helichrysum and country green of linseed and amaranthus. The green carthamus, with its curious orange tufts, acts as a visual bridge between the other materials.

MATERIALS
· · ·
1 bunch dried linseed
· · ·
1 bunch white helichrysum
· · ·
10 stems dried carthamus
· · ·
8 stems large dried orange globe thistle
· · ·
10 stems dried green amaranthus (straight)
· · ·
twine
· · ·
scissors
· · ·
green paper ribbon

The sheaf shape makes a feature of the stems as well as the blooms. Finished with a green ribbon, this decoration would look lovely hung in a country-style kitchen.

1 Set out the materials so that they are easily accessible. Divide each of the bunches of linseed and helichrysum into 10 smaller bunches. Break off the side shoots from the main stems of the carthamus and the globe thistle to increase the number of individual stems available. Take the longest stem of amaranthus in your hand and, to either side of it, add a stem of carthamus and a bunch of linseed making sure all the material is slightly shorter than the amaranthus. The stems of the materials should be spiralled as they are added. Add materials to the bunch to maintain a visual balance between the bold forms of the globe thistle and helichrysum and the more delicate linseed and carthamus.

2 When all the materials have been incorporated, tie with twine at the binding point. Trim the ends of the stems.

3 Make a paper ribbon bow and attach it to the sheaf at the binding point with its tails pointing towards the flowerheads.

JAM-JAR DECORATIONS

· · ·

MATERIALS

· · ·

3 different-shaped jam jars

· · ·

floral adhesive

· · ·

10 skeletonized leaves

· · ·

scissors

· · ·

18 dried yellow rose heads

· · ·

night-light (tea-light) candles

· · ·

1 bunch dried lavender

Containers decorated with plant materials can be very attractive. This type of external embellishment usually conceals a large part of the container so do not waste money buying special pots and vases, just look around the house for something with an interesting shape that you can use.

Here, three different types and sizes of jam jars are decorated for use as night-light (tea light) holders but they could be used to store pens or bric-a-brac or even in the bathroom for toothbrushes, although the damp will accelerate the deterioration of the materials.

Working on this scale does not use a great deal of material and is an opportunity to use left-over items or materials in some way unsuitable for flower arranging. Use your imagination to vary the type of container and the flower decorations.

1 Apply adhesive to the sides of the tallest jam jar (approximately 12 cm (4¾ in) high) and stick five upward-pointing, slightly overlapping skeletonized leaves around the jar flush with its base. Higher up the jam jar glue on a second layer of five overlapping leaves, slightly offset from the first layer, to cover the joins between the leaves.

2 Cut the stems completely off four dried yellow rose heads and glue them to the leaf-covered jar at four equidistant points around the top of its outer surface. Place a night-light (tea-light) candle in the jar.

3 Cut the stems completely off approximately 14 dried yellow rose heads, apply the floral adhesive to the base of each head and stick them around the neck of the second more squat jam jar. Place them tightly together to form a continuous ring of flowers. Put a night-light (tea-light) in the jar.

4 Paste adhesive on to the outside of the third jam jar. Separate the lavender into single stems and stick them vertically to the side of the jar so that the flower spikes project about 1 cm (½ in) above its rim. The flower spikes should be tight to each other to completely cover the sides of the jam jar. Apply a second layer of lavender spikes lower down so that their flowers cover the first layer of stems. Trim the stems projecting below the jam jar flush with its base. Place a night-light (tea-light) in the jar, or use as a small vase.

These decorations would make an unusual centrepiece to a dining table.

RED DISPLAY IN A
GLASS CUBE
· · ·

20 cm (8 in) glass cube

· · ·

20 dried oranges

· · ·

knife

· · ·

*1 block plastic foam for dried
flowers*

· · ·

florist's tape (stem-wrap tape)

· · ·

scissors

· · ·

2 bunches dried bottlebrush

· · ·

*2 bunches dried red-dyed
achillea*

· · ·

*2 bunches dried red-dyed globe
thistle*

· · ·

2 bunches dried red roses

*The display is easy to make
but clever in that the mechanics
of its construction are hidden
when it is completed.*

This display uses dried oranges to create a coloured base within the glass container itself on which an arrangement using only shades of red is built

The arrangement is a dome of massed materials with contrasting textures: the spikes of globe thistles, the velvet cushions of achillea, and the papery petals of roses. The materials and colours are classical but because of the container used the overall effect is very contemporary.

1 Three-quarter fill the glass cube with dried oranges. Cut the plastic foam block so that it fits into the glass cube snugly above the oranges. Only about a third of the depth of the block should be inside the container. Hold the plastic foam securely in place by taping over it and on to the glass (no more than 2.5 cm/1 in down its sides).

2 Cut the bottlebrush stems to 10 cm (4 in) and create the overall outline of the display by pushing their stems into the plastic foam.

3 Cut the dried achillea to a stem length of 10 cm (4 in) and evenly distribute through the bottlebrush by pushing the stems into the foam.

4 Cut the globe thistle stems to 10 cm (4 in) and position evenly throughout the display, pushing their stems into the foam.

5 Cut the dried rose stems to 10 cm (4 in) in length and, in groups of three, fill the remaining spaces evenly throughout the display.

FIREPLACE ARRANGEMENTS
· · ·
MANTELPIECE DISPLAY

MATERIALS
· · ·
knife
· · ·
*1 block plastic foam for dried
flowers*
· · ·
florist's adhesive tape
· · ·
string of hops
· · ·
5 branches glycerined beech
· · ·
3 dried corn cobs
· · ·
12 stems dried sunflowers
· · ·
*12 stems dried green
amaranthus (straight)*

*Using dried flowers is more
practical than a fresh display
because the arrangement will
last far longer and require little
maintenance.*

When a fireplace is not in use it can lose its status as the focal point of a room but decorating its mantelpiece and grate with dramatic floral arrangements will ensure it remains a major feature. The material contents of this mantelpiece arrangement give it a high summer look; it incorporates bright yellow sunflowers, green amaranthus and green hops with corn cobs used as the focal material.

Construction is relatively straightforward provided you maintain the physical as well as visual balance of the display. So, to prevent the arrangement falling forwards make sure the majority of the weight is kept at the back and, whether the plastic foam is in a tray or sitting directly on the mantelpiece make sure it is firmly secured.

1 Cut the block of plastic foam in half, position one half at the centre of the mantelpiece and secure it in place with adhesive tape. If using a plastic tray, first secure the foam to the tray with adhesive tape, then tape the tray to the mantelpiece.

2 Lie the string of hops along the full length of the mantelpiece and secure it to the ends of the shelf with adhesive tape. The hops on the vine should lie on and around the plastic foam without covering it completely.

3 Push the stems of beech into the plastic foam, distributing them evenly to create a domed foliage outline that also trails into the hops. Push the three stems of the corn cobs into the foam towards the back, one at the centre with a slightly shorter cob at either side.

4 Distribute the sunflowers evenly throughout the plastic foam following the domed shape. Place longer stems toward the back and shorter stems towards the front. Arrange the amaranthus throughout the other materials in the plastic foam to reinforce the outline shape.

FIREPLACE GRATE
ARRANGEMENT

· · ·

· · ·

*1½ blocks plastic foam for dried
flowers*

· · ·

scissors

· · ·

8 branches glycerined beech

· · ·

*10 stems dried green
amaranthus (straight)*

· · ·

10 stems dried sunflowers

· · ·

10 stems natural ti tree

*Using dried materials means
that you can make this display
at any time of the year.*

Fill the black hole of an empty grate with a bright display of dried flowers and foliage such as this informal arrangement. The display incorporates the cheery faces of sunflowers with the soft textures of bright green amaranthus and the delicate white flowers of ti tree, all set against the rust tints of beech to create a sunny decoration for a small fireplace.

The plastic foam in this display has been secured by firmly wedging it into the grate. For a larger fireplace the foam will need to be mounted in a separate tray. Do remember that the flowers in a fireplace display are generally arranged to project outwards and preventing it from falling forwards will be the major problem you will encounter.

1 Wedge the plastic foam into the grate. Cut the stems from the branches of glycerined beech and push them into the foam to create a fan-shaped foliage outline that projects out of the grate and forms a curved profile to the front of the display.

2 Push the stems of amaranthus into the foam, distributing them evenly throughout the beech stems to reinforce their outline.

3 Push the sunflower stems into the foam, distributing them evenly throughout the other materials.

4 Push the stems of ti tree in to the foam throughout the display to reinforce the overall shape.

HYDRANGEA CIRCLET
. . .

Hydrangea heads remain beautiful when dried but they do not necessarily dry well when hung in the air. Thus, while it might seem a contradiction in terms, it is best to dry hydrangea whilst they are standing in shallow water. This slows down the process and avoids the hydrangea florets shrivelling.

There is an enormous range of hydrangea colours, from white through pinks, greens, blues and reds to deep purples and in most cases they keep these colours when dried so are ideal for dried flower arranging.

MATERIALS
. . .
12 full dried hydrangea heads
. . .
scissors
. . .
.71 wire
. . .
.32 silver reel (rose) wire
. . .
*1 vine circlet, about 35 cm
(14 in) diameter*

1 Break down each hydrangea head into five smaller florets. Double leg mount each one individually with .71 wire.

2 Take a long length of .32 silver reel (rose) wire and attach a hydrangea floret to the vine circlet by stitching the wire around one of the vines and the wired stem of the hydrangea, pulling tight to secure. Using the same continuous length of wire, add consecutive hydrangea florets in the same way, slightly overlapping them until the front surface of the vine surface is covered.

This circlet is a celebration of the colours of dried hydrangeas and the soft, almost watercolour look, of these hues make it the perfect decoration for the wall of a bedroom.

3 Finish by stitching the silver reel (rose) wire several times around the vine.

MASSED STAR-SHAPED DECORATION

· · ·

MATERIALS

· · ·

*2 blocks plastic foam for dried
flowers*

· · ·

knife

· · ·

star-shaped baking tin

· · ·

scissors

· · ·

50 stems dried lavender

· · ·

100 stems dried yellow roses

*The decoration is simple to
make, although it does call for
a substantial amount of
material.*

This display has a huge visual impact of massed colour and bold shape with the added bonus of the delicious scent of lavender.

Built within a star-shaped baking tin and using yellow and lavender colours, the display has a very contemporary appearance. It would suit a modern style interior.

1 Cut the plastic foam so that it fits neatly into the star-shaped baking tin and is recessed about 2.5 cm (1 in) down from its top. Use the tin as a template for accuracy.

2 Cut the lavender stems to 5 cm (2 in) and group them into fives. Push the groups into the plastic foam all around the outside edge of the star shape to create a border of approximately 1 cm (½ in).

3 Cut the dried roses to 5 cm (2 in). Starting at the points of the star and working towards its centre, push the rose stems into the foam. All the heads should be level with the lavender.

FRUIT AND FUNGI BASKET RIM DECORATION

• • •

Creating a dried flower embellishment for the rim of an old and damaged wicker basket gives it a new lease of life by transforming it into a resplendent container for the display of fruit. The decoration is full of the bold textures and rich colours of sunflowers, oranges, lemons, apples and fungi.

MATERIALS

• • •

45 slices dried orange

• • •

45 slices dried lemon

• • •

45 slices preserved (dried)
apple

• • •

.71 wires

• • •

18 sunflower heads

• • •

16 small pieces dried fungus

• • •

florist's tape (stem-wrap tape)

• • •

scissors

• • •

old wicker basket, without a
handle

• • •

.32 silver reel (rose) wire

1 Group the orange slices in threes and double leg mount each group with .71 wires. Repeat with the lemon and apple slices. Cut the sunflower stems to about 2.5 cm (1 in) and individually double leg mount them on .71 wires. Double leg mount the pieces of fungi with .71 wire. Finally tape over all the wires with florist's tape (stem–wrap tape).

2 Starting at one corner of the basket, bind a group of orange slices to its rim by stitching .32 silver reel (rose) wire through the wicker and around the stem. With the same wire, stitch on the apple slices, the sunflower heads, the lemon slices and the fungi. Repeat this sequence until the rim is covered. Stitch the wire around the last stem and the basket.

The principles of this design can be used to decorate a wicker container of any type.

AUTUMNAL ORANGE DISPLAY
· · ·

MATERIALS
· · ·
3 blocks plastic foam for dried flowers
· · ·
terracotta pot, 30 cm (12 in) high
· · ·
florist's adhesive tape
· · ·
10 stems glycerine-preserved adiantum
· · ·
.71 wires
· · ·
9 dried split oranges
· · ·
scissors
· · ·
10 stems dried carthamus
· · ·
10 stems orange-dyed globe thistles
· · ·
10 stems dried bottlebrush

This is designed as a feature display which would be particularly effective positioned where it could be viewed in the round.

Warm autumn colours dominate this display both in the floral arrangement and in its container. The lovely bulbous terracotta pot is a feature of the display and the arrangement is domed to reflect the roundness of the container. Indeed, in order to focus attention on the pot, the container unusually takes up half the height of the finished display.

The autumnal red and burnt-orange colours of globe thistle, bottlebrush, oranges and adiantum contrast with the green of the carthemus, the orange tufts of which act as a colour link. Texturally varied, the display incorporates tufted flowers, spiky flowers, feathery foliage and recessed leathery skinned fruits.

The arrangement involves simple wiring of the oranges but is otherwise straightforward and just requires a good eye and a little patience in arranging the materials individually in order to achieve the right shape.

1 Pack the blocks of plastic foam into the terracotta pot and secure in place with florist's adhesive tape. The surface of the foam should be about 4 cm (1¼ in) above the rim of the pot.

2 Create a low domed foliage outline using the adiantum stems at their length of about 25 cm (10 in). Wire the dried oranges with .71 wire.

3 Bend down the wires projecting from the bases of the oranges and twist together. Arrange the oranges throughout the adiantum by pushing their wire stems into the foam.

4 Cut the carthamus stems to approximately 25 cm (10 in) and push them into the plastic foam throughout the display to reinforce the height, width and overall shape.

5 Cut the globe thistle stems to a length of approximately 25 cm (10 in) and push them into the foam evenly throughout the display. These are the focal flowers.

6 Finally, cut the stems of bottlebrush to a length of 25 cm (10 in) and push them into the plastic foam to distribute them evenly throughout the display.

DRIED FLOWER TUSSIE MUSSIES

• • •

MATERIALS

• • •

TUSSIE MUSSIE A
scissors

• • •

20 stems dried red roses

• • •

1 bunch dried
Nigella orientalis

• • •

1 bunch dried lavender

• • •

twine

• • •

ribbon

• • •

TUSSIE MUSSIE B
scissors

• • •

20 stems dried pink roses

• • •

half bunch nigella seed heads

• • •

half bunch dried lavender

• • •

half bunch phalaris

• • •

twine

• • •

ribbon

*These tussie mussies are easy
to make, although, to achieve a
satisfactory result, they will use
a lot of material in relation to
their finished size.*

These tussie mussies are made of small spiralled bunches of lavender-scented dried flowers. Embellished with embroidered and velvet ribbon bows, they have a medieval look and would make delightful gifts or could be carried by a young bridesmaid.

1 To make Tussie Mussie A, on the right of the main picture, cut all the materials to a stem length of approximately 18 cm (7 in). Set out all the materials in separate groups for easy access. Start by holding a single rose in your hand and add the other materials one by one.

2 Add, in turn, stems of *Nigella orientalis,* lavender and rose to the central stem. Continue this sequence, all the while turning the bunch in your hand to ensure that the stems form a spiral. Hold the growing bunch about two-thirds of the way down the stems.

3 When all the materials are in place, secure the bunch by tying twine around the binding point of the stems. Trim the bottoms of the stems even. Tie a ribbon around the binding point and finish in a neat bow. (Follow the same method for Tussie Mussie B).

FOUR SEASONS IN A BASKET

. . .

This contemporary massed display in a circular basket is divided into quarters, each representing – by its material content and colours – one of the four seasons. It is important to keep the materials tightly massed together for maximum effect.

MATERIALS

. . .

knife

. . .

*2 blocks plastic foam for dried
flowers*

. . .

round shallow basket

. . .

florist's adhesive tape

. . .

scissors

. . .

60 stems dried natural phalaris

. . .

17 stems cream helichrysum

. . .

40 dried deep pink roses

. . .

160 stems dried lavender

. . .

25 stems carthamus

. . .

*5 stems preserved (dried)
brown adiantum*

. . .

10 cinnamon sticks

. . .

5 dried oranges with splits

. . .

71 wires

1 Cut the plastic foam to fit and wedge it in the basket. Divide the surface of the foam into quarters by making a cross with adhesive tape. Cut the stems of phalaris and helichrysum to a length of about 6 cm (2½ in). Group the phalaris stems in fives and arrange them evenly throughout one quarter of the basket. Distribute the helichrysum among the phalaris with all the heads at the same level.

Cut the stems of the roses to 6 cm (2½ in) and the lavender to an overall length of 7 cm (2¾ in). Group the lavender stems in fives and arrange them in the second quarter of the basket. Push the rose stems into the foam, throughout the lavender.

Cut the stems of carthamus to 6 cm (2½ in). Break fronds of adiantum from the main stems and cut them to 7 cm (2¾ in). Push the carthamus stems into the foam throughout the third quarter of the basket.

Distribute the adiantum evenly among the carthamus, keeping them tight together.

Cut the sticks of cinnamon to 6 cm (2½ in). Single leg mount the dried oranges and cut the protruding wires to a length of 4 cm (1½ in). Push the wires of the oranges into the foam to arrange them evenly throughout the fourth quarter of the basket. Push the cinnamon sticks into the foam, massing them tightly between the dried oranges.

Involving only a small amount of wiring, the display is not difficult to make but is an excellent exercise in massing dried flowers and would make a powerful centrepiece for a circular table.

PINK BASKET
DISPLAY

· · ·

MATERIALS

· · ·

knife

· · ·

*1 block plastic foam for dried
flowers*

· · ·

*oval basket, about 20 cm
(8 in) long*

· · ·

florist's adhesive tape

· · ·

scissors

· · ·

*20 stems dried red amaranthus
(straight)*

· · ·

20 stems dried deep pink roses

· · ·

*20 stems deep pink
helichrysum*

The natural deep pink hues of these roses, helichrysum and amaranthus have survived the preservation process and here work together to produce a richly-coloured dense textural display of dried flowers.

The arrangement, mounted in an oval basket, is a low dome and thus would be good as a table arrangement, but its lavish formal appearance would make it appropriate to any reception room in the house.

1 Cut the block of plastic foam to fit snugly into the basket and fix it securely in place with adhesive tape.

2 Cut the amaranthus to an overall length of 14 cm (5¾ in) and push them into the plastic foam to create a dome-shaped outline.

3 Cut the stems of dried roses to a length of 12 cm (4¾ in) and push them into the foam, distributing them evenly throughout the amaranthus.

4 Cut 10 of the helichrysum stems to approximately 12 cm (4¾ in) in length and push them into the foam evenly throughout the display. Cut the other 10 stems to approximately 10 cm (4 in) in length and push them into the foam evenly throughout the display, so that they are recessed to give visual depth to the arrangement.

The materials in the display have nicely contrasting textures: papery helichrysum, roses and velvet-spiked amaranthus.

85

CINNAMON AND
ORANGE RING

· · ·

MATERIALS

· · ·

glue gun and glue sticks

· · ·

5 dried oranges

· · ·

*plastic foam ring for dried
flowers, 13 cm (5¾ in)
diameter.*

· · ·

20 cinnamon sticks

*This lovely ring would make
an ideal gift – perhaps as a
house-warming present, or for
someone who loves cooking.*

The warm colours, spicy smell and culinary content of this small decorated
ring make it perfect for the wall of a kitchen.

The display is not complicated to make but requires nimble fingers to handle
the very small pieces of cinnamon used. These pieces have to be tightly packed
together to achieve the right effect and great care must be taken because attaching
so much cinnamon to the plastic foam may cause it to collapse. To help avoid this
happening you can glue the foam ring to stiff card cut to the same outline, before
starting work.

1 Apply glue to the bases
of the dried oranges
and fix them to the plastic
foam ring, equally spaced
around it. Break the
cinnamon sticks into 2-4
cm (¾-1½ in) pieces.

2 Apply glue to the
bottom of the pieces of
cinnamon and push them
into the foam between the
dried oranges, keeping
them close together to
achieve a massed effect.

3 Glue a line of the
cinnamon pieces
around both the inside and
outside edges of the ring
to cover the plastic foam
completely.

CLASSIC ORANGE AND CLOVE POMANDER
· · ·

This classic pomander starts as fresh material that, as you use it, dries into a beautiful old-fashioned decoration with a warm spicy smell evocative of mulled wine and the festive season.

Make several pomanders using different ribbons and display them in a bowl, hang them around the house, use them as Christmas decorations or even hang them in your wardrobe.

MATERIALS
· · ·
3 small firm oranges
· · ·
3 types of ribbon
· · ·
scissors
· · ·
cloves

Pomanders are easy and fun to make, and ideal as gifts. Remember to tighten the ribbons as the pomanders dry and shrink.

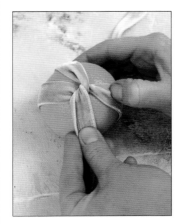

1 Tie a ribbon around an orange, crossing it over at the base.

2 Finish off at the top of the orange by tying the ribbon into a bow. Adjust the position of the ribbon as necessary to ensure the orange is divided into four equal-sized areas.

3 Starting at the edges of the areas, push the sharp ends of the exposed cloves into the orange skin and continue until each quarter is completely covered.

CLASSICAL URN

· · ·

A lovely shallow urn in rust-tinged cast iron is the inspiration for this display. The classic shape of the container is a major feature of the display and is echoed by a dried flower arrangement of traditional elegance.

Predominantly white and yellow, with contrasting greens, the display is a dense dome of roses, honesty, ti tree, eucalyptus, linseed and phalaris.

MATERIALS

· · ·

knife

· · ·

2 blocks plastic foam for dried flowers

· · ·

cast-iron urn

· · ·

florist's adhesive tape

· · ·

scissors

· · ·

10 stems preserved eucalyptus

· · ·

10 stems bleached honesty

· · ·

2 bunches linseed

· · ·

2 bunches natural phalaris

· · ·

20 stems dried white roses

· · ·

1 bunch natural ti tree

1 Cut the blocks of plastic foam to fit into the cast iron urn and wedge it in, securing it with adhesive tape.

2 Cut the eucalyptus stems to 15 cm (6 in) long and push them into the plastic foam to create an even domed foliage outline.

3 Cut the honesty stems to about 20 cm (8 in) in length and push them into the plastic foam, distributing them throughout the foliage with longer stems towards the centre of the urn.

4 Separate the linseed into 18 smaller bunches, each cut to a length of 15 cm (6 in). Push the bunches into the plastic foam evenly throughout the other materials.

The luminosity of the arrangement's pale colours would lighten a dark corner of a room.

5 Cut the phalaris and the rose stems to approximately 15 cm (6 in) in length and individually push into the plastic foam evenly throughout the display.

6 Cut the ti tree stems to approximately 15 cm (6 in) in length and arrange them evenly throughout the display.

RED TIED SHEAF

· · ·

50 stems dried lavender

· · ·

10 stems Protea compacta
buds

· · ·

10 stems natural ti tree

· · ·

15 stems dried red roses

· · ·

twine

· · ·

scissors

· · ·

satin ribbon, 5 cm (2 in)

*The demanding aspect of the
construction of the sheaf is the
technique of spiralling the
materials in your hand. But
this display is relatively small,
which simplifies the task.*

A tied sheaf of flowers arranged in the hand makes an attractive and informal wall decoration. To make a successful wall hanging, the sheaf must be made with a flat back, while at the same time it should have a profiled front to add visual interest. With such exotic colours, this is a display that would work best in an interior decorated with rich colours and furnishings.

1 Lay out the materials so that they are easily accessible and separate the lavender into 10 smaller groups. Hold the longest protea in your hand, and behind it add a slightly longer stem of ti tree, then hold rose stems to either side of the protea, both slightly shorter than the first. Continue adding materials in a regular repeating sequence to the growing bunch in your hand, spiralling the stems as you do so.

2 When all the materials have been used, tie the sheath with twine at the binding point. Trim the stems so that they make up about one-third of the overall length of the sheaf.

3 To finish the display make a separate ribbon bow and attach it to the sheaf at the binding point.

ROSE AND CLOVE POMANDER
. . .

This pomander is a decadent display of rose heads massed in a ball. But it has a secret: cloves hidden between the rose heads which give the pomander its lasting spicy perfume.

It relies for its impact on the use of large quantities of tightly packed flowers, all of the same type and colour.

MATERIALS
. . .
ribbon 40 x 2.5 cm
(16 x 1 in)
. . .
.71 wire
. . .
plastic foam ball for dried
flowers, approximately 10 cm
(4 in) diameter
. . .
scissors
. . .
100 stems dried roses
. . .
200 cloves

1 Fold the ribbon in half and double leg mount its cut ends together with a .71 wire. To form a ribbon handle, push the wires right through the plastic foam ball so that they come out the other end, and pull the projecting wires so that the double leg mounted part of the ribbon becomes firmly embedded in the plastic foam. Turn the excess wire back into the foam.

Almost profligate in its use of materials, this pomander is quick to make and would be a wonderful and very special gift.

2 Cut the stems of the dried rose heads to a length of approximately 2.5 cm (1 in). Starting at the top of the plastic foam ball, push the stems of the dried rose heads into the foam to form a tightly packed circle around the base of the ribbon handle. As you work push a clove into the plastic foam between each rose head. Continue forming concentric circles of rose heads and cloves around the plastic foam ball until it is completely covered.

91

CRESCENT MOON WREATH

· · ·

MATERIALS
· · ·

35 Craspedia globosa *heads*

· · ·

scissors

· · ·

.38 silver wires

· · ·

1 bunch dried linseed

· · ·

florist's tape (stem-wrap tape)

· · ·

.71 wires

This novelty decoration is designed to be hung on the wall of a nursery or child's bedroom. The golden-yellow of *Craspedia globosa* and the pale gold sheen of the linseed seed heads give the decoration a luminosity which children will love.

It is made like a garland headdress, on a stay wire but shaped to the outline of a crescent rather than a circle.

1 Cut the *Craspedia globosa* heads to a stem length of approximately 2 cm (¾ in) and double leg mount them on .38 silver wires. Split the dried linseed into very small bunches, each approximately 4 cm (1¾ in) long, and double leg mount them on .38 wires. Tape all the wired materials with the florist's tape (stem–wrap tape). Create a stay wire about 60 cm (24 in) long from the .71 wire.

2 Cover the stay wire with florist's tape (stem–wrap tape) Bend the stay wire into the outline of a crescent shape, taking care to ensure an even arc and pointed ends.

3 At one open end of the stay wire, tape on a bunch of linseed, followed by a small head of the *Craspedia globosa* slightly overlapping. Use the smaller heads of the *Craspedia globosa* at the pointed ends of the crescent and the larger heads at its centre. As you get towards the centre of the crescent, increase the width of the line of materials by adding material to the sides of the wire. Decrease the width again as you work towards the far point.

4 When the outside edge of the crescent outline has been completed, repeat the process on the inner edge but this time working from the bent point of the crescent down towards the open end of the stay wire. When the inner wire has been decorated, join the two open ends of the stay wire by taping them together, then cut off any excess wires and tape over their ends. This joint will be hidden by the dried materials.

To make the crescent shape accurately – narrower at its points – requires a degree of skill and like all wired decorations, time and patience.

INDEX

• • •

AUTHOR'S ACKNOWLEDGEMENTS

THE AUTHOR WOULD LIKE TO THANK ROGER EGERICKX AND
RICHARD KISS OF DESIGN AND DISPLAY (SALES LTD) FOR THEIR
GENEROUS PROVISION OF FACILITIES

WITH SPECIAL THANKS TO JENNY BENNETT FOR ALL HER HARD WORK.